CU00691393

SONG OF THE COSMOS

SONG OF THE COSMOS

An Introduction to Traditional Cosmology

Arthur Versluis

PRISM · UNITY

This book is dedicated to René Guénon, Titus Burckhardt and Frithjof Schuon.

Published in Great Britain 1991 by

PRISM PRESS
2 South Street
Bridport
Dorset DT6 3NQ

Distributed in the USA by
AVERY PUBLISHING GROUP
120 Old Broadway
Garden City Park
NY 11040

Published in Australia by
UNITY PRESS
Lindfield
NSW 2070

ISBN 1 85327 065 2

Typeset by Prism Press, Bridport, Dorset.
Printed by The Guernsey Press Ltd, The Channel Islands.

Contents

Introduction

This book is reconstructive: it is intended to reconstitute — so far as is possible for those of us born into a world hostile to any understanding which reaches beyond the material realm — something of what mankind has understood for millennia. Until the modern era in the West — beginning roughly in the eighteenth century — mankind lived in the light of the received scriptures and traditions.

Even today there are many who, in the face of a hostile world that drowns in a flood of anti-traditional ideas, still hold to the traditional understanding of the cosmos as understood by their ancestors. In this study I will discuss the nature of traditional cosmologies, offering this work to modern readers in the hope that, for at least a few, it will act as a reminder of the truth, as an incentive to embrace and to embody authentic traditions.

Of course, clearly there are many religions upon this earth, many received scriptures, and these do not apparently agree on certain points — so it will be objected that when we speak of 'traditional cosmology' there are many cosmologies, not just one. This is true, in a limited sense: one cannot, for instance, at first glance find in Christianity beings corresponding to the 'six kinds of beings' in Buddhism. But on closer inspection, one does find correspondences to the Buddhist understanding in Christianity: the *pretas*, or 'hungry ghosts' correspond to certain beings in purgatory; the hell-being, animal, and human realms are the same in both traditions and self-explanatory; the *devas* correspond in certain respects to the Christian Angels; and the *asuras* and the Titans, or Fallen Angels, are virtually identical. So although it may appear that the various traditions are divergent, even irreconcilable, this is not so: fundamentally, the world's traditions agree.

This agreement is only natural: the truth is naturally unitary, and if man in Germany understands that there are, say, Angelic beings, is it surprising that man in Tibet, or in Russia or in the American prairies or anywhere else should also recognise there are such beings? More surprising is modern man's ignorance of, and even hostile denial of such beings' existence; in many respects, modern man is much more ignorant of traditional cosmology than the most 'unlearned' of peasants. We should be surprised, not that traditional cosmological doctrines are unitary, but rather that we have forgotten them.

There is an additional factor in the unity of traditional cosmology: primordiality. All the world's received traditions are reflections of a primordial tradition; the correspondences in all the cosmological doctrines of the world religions result not from horizontal 'influence' (Nestorian missions being responsible for Tibetan Buddhism, say, as certain zealous Christians held in the nineteenth century), but from vertical inheritance, being as they are akin to the branches and leaves of a tree with a single trunk. That trunk is rooted above, not below, and its branches are revelations.

It is commonplace nowadays to reduce traditional cosmological doctrines to mere psychology. Modern man can perhaps accept that there are Angels, a heaven or a hell, if these realities are viewed as psychological and hence relative. But this psychologising of reality is merely a caricature of the traditional teachings. These hold that man can, by virtue of the centrality of his station in the cosmos, through meditative transmutation experience the various other stations of being. That man is a microcosm does not mean that there is no macrocosm, that the subjective being is the only reality.

Psychology does not explain everything; to be trapped

in psychology is not the way to liberation. All traditional cosmology exists for a purpose: it offers mankind an understanding of the cosmos in order that he be able, through a religious path, to transcend the cosmological.[1] Man exists, and can only exist, in a cosmos: beneath manifestation is the manifest Substance, and above manifestation are the transcendent stations, beyond which is absolute increate Transcendence. Man can sink into the infernal and dissolve, or he can ascend into the transcendent states, transcending the human state entirely: and traditional cosmology exists in order that he beware the former, and enter into the latter.

This is not to say, however, that man is 'evolving' toward some 'universal religion', as various nineteenth-and even twentieth-century writers have thought. Were all the world's religions moving toward a single religion, this surely would have been prophesied — but in the world's scriptures, one finds instead a consistent emphasis upon the decline into irreligion and upon the chaos and destruction which attends the end of a timecycle. We have been given the various traditions, which have in turn flowered. One cannot say whether they have crystallised, all of them, into their final forms, for *spiritus autem ubi vult spirat*: 'the spirit bloweth where it listeth'. But though there are certain advocates of a 'dialogue' between Hinduism and Christianity, or Buddhism and Christianity, say, there is no evidence whatever of an 'evolving universal religion'.

In this work, my aim is simply to offer the reader a general understanding of traditional cosmological doctrines, keeping in mind both the unities, and the divergences of the various traditions from which I shall draw. 'Heaven' in the Christian sense seems quite different from the same concept as it appears in, say, Buddhism, or again in Hinduism, and to ignore such apparent differences is to do as much injustice to the tradition as to deny that, fundamentally, the given tradition is a reflection of the primordial truth it certainly offers. We can neither ignore divergences, nor deny fundamental unity.

First, we will discuss cosmic centrality and the human station, moving second to infernal or sub-human realms, third to non-human or peripheral stations, and then finally to transcendent, or supra-human stations. The aim here, again, is not merely to sketch doctrines which man once believed, but which are no longer 'relevant'; rather, our aim is to give a concise overview of traditional cosmology in order that — seeing the vistas of traditional understanding as perhaps he has never before seen them — the reader will be motivated to turn toward that tradition to which he or she is most naturally drawn, to enter into the mysteries perchance here glimpsed.

If this is so for even a few, this book will have fulfilled its purpose; and with this in mind, we begin.

Chapter I
The Nature of the Earth

In the modern view, the earth is simply the result of more or less random 'evolution' over a long period of time. According to this view, the earth is not sacred — the most some scientists seem to manage these days is to believe that the earth forms a whole, or a biosphere, an intricate network which they call Gaia, using the ancient Greek word. Even this concept receives mockery from some quarters as, in some cases, well it should.[2] But in all traditional cultures, the earth is regarded as sacred because it is the direct manifestation of spiritual principles, 'imprinted' in it and in us. The earth is sacred not because it has evolved by chance, but because it reflects the Divine, and traditional religion is our means of realising this.

Everything in the cosmos exists because it bears the imprint of the Divine. This the Hau de no sau nee tribes expressed as follows:

> We believe that all living things are spiritual beings. Spirits can be expressed as energy forms manifested in matter. A blade of grass is an energy form manifested in matter — grass matter. The spirit of the grass is that unseen force which produces the species of grass, and it is manifest to us in the form of real grass.[3]

So too the wood, the stones, the air, the water, the fire, and the animals around us are all spiritual beings manifesting in matter. These spiritual beings are in medieval Christian alchemical thought called 'elementals' — that is, living beings manifesting in earth, in water, in fire and in air. These beings do not possess human consciousness, but they possess a certain kind of consciousness, to be sure.

As C.S. Lewis noted in his *The Discarded Image*, there must needs be a third force between two forces, linking them together; and this third force is in medieval Christian understanding, the daemonic realm.[4] The daemonic links the natural and the divine, man and the gods. The daemonic takes many forms: there are 'good daemons', or Angels, which mediate between God and man, bestowing their apportionment of divine beneficence upon the human realm; there are the 'fallen daemons', who have become perverted and self-seeking, destructive and wrathful; and there are the 'elemental spirits' manifesting everywhere in nature.

Said Plato, in his *Timaeus*, the Divine intended to make a 'moving image of Eternity', and consequently:

> we must not call the mother and receptacle of visible and sensible things either earth or air or fire or water, nor yet any of their compounds or components, but we shall not be wrong if we describe it as invisible and formless, all-embracing, possessed in a most puzzling way of intelligibility, yet very hard to grasp. And so far as we can arrive at its nature, from what we have said, the most accurate description would be to say that the part of it which has become fiery appears as fire, the part which has become wet appears as water, and other parts appear as earth and air in so far as they respectively come to resemble them.[5]

There is one spiritual energy, but there are countless manifestations of it.

In traditional thought — Greek here, but also in Hindu, Buddhist, medieval Christian, tribal Indian and others — there is no great divide between the Divine and the earthly. Rather, the earthly, the natural *is* the Divine in a certain mysterious hypostasis. There is, in other words, an hierarchy of existence, and the natural world is part of that hierarchy, bearing therefore the 'stamp' of the Divine. Everything in the cosmos must necessarily reflect its Creator, or Divine origin.

To say this is not to espouse pantheism, for pantheism is merely a modern misunderstanding of the traditional mystery of God's omnipresence. To say that this stick reflects Divine reality is not to say that this stick is God, even though in a certain sense this is true, as Meister Eckhart said. On a temporal level, one cannot but say that the stick is a stick, the tree is a tree, man is man, and God is God. But from an ultimate point of view, one cannot help but acknowledge that this stick as it is in God is higher than an angel as it would be outside of God, that indeed in its fundamental nature as part of Divine creation the stick has its origin in God and therefore in an ultimate sense is indivisible from God, as is everything in creation.

The Qabalistic view, which has its parallels in certain Islamic sects, is also that in a mysterious way, God separates Himself from Himself, in order that there can be 'space' for Creation. Says Gershom Scholem on this doctrine of *tsim-tsum*:

> The starting point of this theory is the idea that the very essence of *Ein-Sof* leaves no space whatsoever for creation, for it is impossible to imagine an area which is not already God, since this would constitute a limitation of His Infinity ... Consequently, an act of creation is possible only through the entry of God into Himself, that is, through an act of *tsim-tsum*, whereby He contracts Himself, and so makes it possible for something which is not *Ein-Sof* to exist. Some part of the Godhead therefore withdraws and leaves room, so to speak, for the creative processes to come into play. Such a retreat must precede any emanation.[6]

Everything in creation bears the Divine imprint, but is in a mysterious way 'freed' to the possibilities of manifestation by Divine self-contraction.

A related doctrine is to be found in the Upaniṣads, as when in the Brihad Aranyaka Upanisad we read that in order for creation to take place, the Atman had to split (*pat*) into two pieces.[7] This corresponds to human generation as well, for there must be a 'splitting apart' of the One before there can be an engendering. And at precisely this point we touch upon the mystery of the Fall and the Redemption of creation, to use Christian terms. All creation is 'rent asunder' by virtue of its very existence. The very nature of existence is dualistic, and this primal division then emanates throughout all levels of the hierarchy. All beings are by virtue of their existence separated from their Divine origin even while surrounded by and in a real sense a manifestation of it. This is the Fall, and the task of man as a microcosm is to restore Divine unity to the world, to 'raise up' creation to its original unity. Every man participates in the action of Divine Redemption, or in the action of the Fall.

The existence of Evil bespeaks our fallen condition; for evil riddles the human and natural worlds. As the Christian theologian Franz von Baader said, all nature carries in itself the signs of unimaginable catastrophes. The Fall was not merely a single, primal division, but a metaphysical, and then a cosmological splintering asunder; for whenever the process of Divine contraction was begun, it was inevitable that it have as one conclusion the manifestation of evil, as part of the playing out of possibilities. This cosmological manifestation is far greater than anything the human being can comprehend; for everything in our present world is attenuated, 'narrowed' by virtue of its earthly nature, whereas the battle between evil and good which we are discussing takes place on a metaphysical and then cosmological scale far vaster than the merely human.[8]

But it is given to man, by virtue of his central place in the cosmos, to be a redeemer of Nature. This function — man as redeemer — is why elemental beings surrounding us, in trees, in stones, in the water and air have spiritual significance to us. For one human function is to recognise and to elevate those beings, to assimilate and to transmute them. Man alone has the capacity to 'bridge the worlds' as a microcosm, or mirror of the cosmos. And this bridging means that man as divine vice-regent upon earth can join heaven and earth, can reveal the mineral, the plant and the animal in its spiritual significance, in a real sense 'justifying' it.

We can see this function within traditional cultures manifesting in the healer, who uses 'ordinary' plants, minerals, and animal products to heal the wounded or the ill. The plant, mineral or animal product used in a religious healing acts to heal a human being by restoring an elemental balance within him. But in that very assimilation and healing the plant or other substance is 'raised up' and justified by the human being with whom it is joined. This is why eating meat is justifiable within certain cultures as well: the animal being killed and eaten in a ritual manner, is assimilated into the human sphere, and thereby 'raised up'.

All of this is true only within a traditional culture, and with reference to a religious or spiritual man, who by virtue of that spirituality is able to transmute the world around him, to assimilate it into the Divine sphere and into the primordial harmony which was lost by the Fall. This is why the Sufis say that the whole of creation exists for the *qutb*, or saint, the Pole of the world: the religious culture of which he is the pinnacle transmutes all that it touches and includes, raising it up into its original spiritual significance once again. The function of religion on this earth is to return man to that state of beatitude which was his before the Fall, and is his always if he but knew it. And by virtue of this redemption of man, all of creation is also redeemed, insofar as it is also of a spiritual origin.

Traditional medicine is indivisible from the religion of which it is but one reflection; and this is why modern forms of herbalism, say, or other kinds of once-traditional medicine work only in attenuated ways, if at all. Divorced from their spiritual meaning and function, herbalism is merely another technical means of 'fixing' someone's body, rather than a restoration of primordial balance and an influx of transcendent power.[9]

In a traditional culture, everything in Nature bespeaks its celestial origin; the culture is a means of restoring to the world its transcendent significance in human eyes. In a fallen world, the otter is simply an otter, the bear a bear. But in the restored world, the paradisal world, the otter and the bear are manifestations of spiritual archetypes.[10] And so it is with everything in Nature. A star is not simply a star, but part of a nexus of archetypal symbolism, connected in some way to the symbolism of an archetypal animal or other being.

What is more, the traditional culture acts as a vehicle for this restoration of meaning to the world; it takes stone, or wood, or animals, and ideally restores them in human eyes to their archetypal meaning. Wood, for example, which is consecrated and used in the building of a simple beautiful Shinto temple in the mountains, is realised in its archetypal form within the shrine. This is not to say that all trees should be so used — of course not. Most trees are left untouched — but this one tree had its 'woodness' realised within the temple. It is a part of a tree, but something more than that as well.

By way of contrast, consider 'wood products' made in the modern world. A tree is dragged out of the forest with all its brethren, chipped up into tiny pieces by massive machines, glued together, pressed, molded and sent away as, say, molded desks, or boards, or whatever. Here the wood is reduced to something less than wood, made into the facsimile of wood: it can have no sacred qualities left. It is merely, and in the worst sense of the word, an 'object'. Far from having been 'raised up', the tree has been 'thrown down', or 'thrown away'.

This process of 'uniformation', if we may so call it, is precisely the inverse of the traditional culture, which seeks to recognise in every living thing its archetypal qualities. We have, many of us, heard of the American Indian tribal tradition of eating that portion of a creature which we might wish to assimilate. For intelligence, one might eat the brain, for strength, the liver or heart, and so forth. This is an instance of recognising archetypal qualities — though there is much more to such a practise than simply that outlined above. As Marsilio Ficino, the Renaissance Platonist, wrote: the 'foods we eat properly, though they are not alive in themselves, return us to the form of our life through our spirit,' and hence 'If you want food to take form for your brain, liver, or stomach, you should eat, as much as you can, food such as brains, livers, and stomachs of animals not far distant from human nature.'[11]

But Ficino goes on to complete more of the picture:

> If you want your body and spirit to receive power from some limb of the world, for example from the Sun, learn which are the Solar things among metals and stones, even more among plants, but among the animal world most of all, especially among men. For there is no doubt that they confer on you similar qualities. These and more should be held forth and taken inside for their powers, especially on a day and in an hour of the Sun, with the Sun reigning in its figure in the sky. Solar things are all those things called Heliotrope ... for example, gold ... chrysolite, carbuncle, myrrh, incense, musk, amber ... the lion, the beetle, the crocodile, people who are golden-haired, curly-haired, sometimes baldheaded, and the magnanimous.[12]

This quotation from Ficino gives some indication of the wider implications the 'doctrine of sympathy' possesses: for one can take the doctrine very far indeed. There are solar, venusian, martial, jovial, saturnine, mercurial and lunar correspondences running throughout all of Nature, woven like threads or like the colours refracted through a prism. And by assimilating them into one's life, according to the proper balances and patterns, one can not only live in a more balanced way, but will transmit this balance to the world around one. Agriculture, artisanry, building, cooking — all the arts by which mankind lives, can be patterned according to celestial and planetary balances, the purpose of which is to return us to a paradisal state of balance, a state 'closer' to the Divine archetypal realm.

This balancing is the process of redemption going on in the world on a cultural level. Said the 'unknown philosopher' Louis Claude de St. Martin: 'As proof that we are regenerated, we must regenerate all around us.'[13] This law applies alike to the saint, and to the culture of which he is the manifestation. Except for special revelation, culture is the only means we have of realising the true nature of our world; it is the mesocosm between man the microcosm, and the cosmos as a whole.[14] Larger than man as individual, culture is the means by which he comes to know the true nature of his world. Culture is simply the application, or physical manifestation, of religious tradition.

Through religious tradition do we come to know the spiritual significances of our world. Man bears within him an intuitive knowledge of archetypal meanings, but religious tradition brings this knowledge to the forefront of consciousness, and makes it part of everyday life. We know in our heart the symbolism of the lotus or of the rose — but only when these are part of our religious tradition, imbued with all the power and mystery of ages of worship, do their higher significances become clearer to us.

In this bringing to consciousness, intellect as ordinarily conceived, as ratiocination, has only a limited function. One comes to know symbolism by living its meanings, by having symbolic meanings permeate through our lives, into both deeper and higher levels than what we moderns call mind. We may 'know' intellectually what it means to prostrate ourselves, to genuflect, or to close the hands together in the reverential gesture of *gassho*[15] — but only when the actual gesture of humility is ingrained completely into our entire being, do we *know* what it means.

This knowing on every level is indivisible from our being here upon this earth as humans: man, as is traditionally said, joins heaven and earth. But he can only do so when he is a vehicle for the Divine. And this knowing is ours only as a gift: we are given it not for our own aggrandizement, but that we in turn may give.

When we fully understand this truth, in the depths of our being, the interwoven symbolism, the meanings of all things in Nature will be opened to us. For this true knowledge is ours only if we can approach it in true humility, if we are prepared to receive it through a true teacher, and standing within a tradition which can protect both the knowledge and we ourselves.

Man was meant to live, not isolated, but as restorer of his world to its original pristine condition. He was meant to live in a world perpetually revealing to him new depths and heights of meaning, new insights, new life, and constantly evoking his gratitude. Nature in her primordial splendor bespeaks this to us each moment but we, intent upon some goal or other, upon some use for her creatures, do not see these truths — we rush by them, caught in the currents of our own ratiocination, or in emotional eddies. If we can be still, if we can but let Nature speak to us in silence and in contemplation of her mysteries, we can yet learn the nature of this our earth. There is and always shall be time for that, if we are but open.

The Tree of the Soul. A figure attributed to William Law, found in The Works of Jacob Behmen *(London, 1764-81), showing the transcendent light above, the paradisal realm at the top of the tree, the 'fire world', the 'dark world' and, in the foreground, the 'solar world' of man.*

Chapter II
The Axis of the Worlds
and the Human Station

As above, so below: so reads the maxim in the *Tabula Smaragdina*, or Emerald Tablet of the Hermetists. This symbolism recurs in every tradition; it is in fact inherent in the human psyche itself. We naturally think of earth as below heaven, and of the Pit as below earth. Of course, the Hermetic maxim 'as above, so below' refers not only to an axial symbolism, but to a correspondence between the different realms arrayed on a vertical axis. What exists on earth is a reflection of heaven; what exists in hell is a reflection of what exists on earth. Nonetheless, this vertical symbolism naturally means that each degree on the axis downward is more distant from the inconceivable Light from which all below originated. This axial symbolism is to be found in Buddhism, in Christianity, indeed in every tradition and, in different ways, is central to all of them.

In Isaiah 14:12ff. we read of Lucifer, leader of the Fallen Angels, (the Nephilim):

How you are fallen from heaven,
O Day Star, son of Dawn!
How you are cut down to the ground, you who laid the
nations low!
You said in your heart,
'I will ascend to heaven;
above the stars of God
I will set my throne on high
I will sit on the mount of assembly
in the far north; I will ascend above the heights of the

clouds
I will make myself like the Most High'.
But you are brought down to Sheol,
to the depths of the Pit.

This verse refers at once to any man who seeks to exalt himself above all the nations, but this only by virtue of its primal reference, which is to those Angels who, having fallen and become Titanic, seek to rise up against the Holy One and to usurp the Holy Throne of the Assembly. Any man who so acts is but reflecting the archetypal attempts of the Fallen Angels to lay siege to Heaven, to the North. Yet to completely understand the meaning of this passage — and of correlate passages in the Vedas, in the Upaniṣads, in the Buddhist Sutras and in the Norse Eddas, as well as in Taoist and Amerindian or aboriginal legend — we must first understand the axial symbolism which is inherent in them all.

But we must keep in mind that the Old Testament and to some extent the New Testament represent attenuated or encoded teachings. In the Maitri Upanisad, for instance, the nature of the World-Axis is made explicitly clear, and we read that 'The threefold Brahman has his root above, His branches being space, air, fire, water, earth, and the rest. This is the One Fig-tree (*eka asvattha*) and therein lies the fiery energy (*tejas*) of the Supernal Sun'.[16] In the passage from Isaiah, the references to the World-Axis which stretches from the pit to the heavens are implicit; their cosmological implications must be pointed out.

This implicit-ness of the Judaic revelation has to do with its limited nature more generally: it refers, after all, to only part of one timecycle,[17] and to the 'chosen people', and whereas the Christian revelation represents an opening out to all mankind, it too refers only to one part of a timecycle.[18] In Buddhist and Hindu teachings, for instance — and in certain Amerindian traditions like the Hopi as well[19] — time is understood as consisting in vast cycles, of which 'history' in a Judaeo-Christian sense is only a tiny segment. As a result of this focus in the

Judaeo-Christian view of the cosmos, it is often useful to consider scriptures from these traditions with Hindu, Buddhist or other traditions in mind, for they may bring out meanings otherwise overlooked.

We may point out first, then, the vertical nature of the symbolism: Lucifer wishes to usurp the throne 'on high', but is brought 'down' to the pit. The 'mount of the assemblies' is in the North, and Sheol, or the Pit of the dead, is in the South. Elsewhere I have discussed in some detail the Taoist symbolism of the North and of the Gate of Life in the Northeast,[20] and its connections with the Vedic symbolism of the *devayana* and *pitryana*.[21] Here it is only necessary to say that both in Taoist and in Buddhist cosmology, as in the Vedic and pre-Vedic symbolism, the North is seen as the Gateway of the Sun or the Gateway of Life; in the North is the *devayana*, or Pathway of the Gods, while in the South is the *pitryana*, or Pathway of the Fathers, or Ancestors. When a being after death travels the *devayana*, he passes through the Gateway of the Sun and 'transcends the cosmos'; whereas if a being travels the *pitryana*, his course is only sublunary and he returns again to the human realm.

This symbolism may well seem arbitrary until we consider that the earth revolves around a central axis which, from the human perspective, is inevitably marked by the Sun, with all its attendant symbolism of light and of life. This axis is Northward; the earth turns in a clockwise direction around this Pole, and so even though from any point on the turning globe directional orientation appears to change, from a distanced point of view, the symbolism remains absolutely constant. From any point on the rotational circumference, North remains cosmologically inward toward the Pole.

As a result, we can see why — and in this discussion, we must recall that we are no longer speaking merely in terms of a materialistic cosmos, but of a cosmos as expression of spiritual reality — the path toward heaven is North 'toward the sun-gate', or toward the Gate to the Cosmos, whereas the Path of the Fathers is to the South,

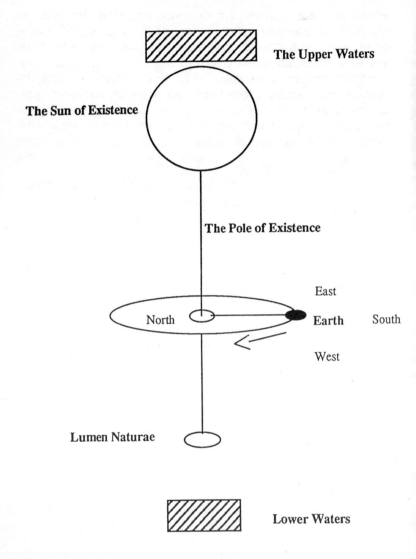

The Pole of Existence. The earth orbits around the world-axis, and thus northward is also 'inward' toward the Pole, and toward union with the celestial light of the Sun of existence. In this sense, to move toward the Pole is also to 'ascend'.

which is to say, away from the Sun, and therefore part of the cycle of blindness which extends from the earth to the moon and back. The function of religious tradition is to properly orient man so that he can ascend the 'axis of the worlds', which is to say — in the inherent unity of cosmological and spiritual symbolism which always holds in cosmological doctrines — to transmute consciousness in such a way as to realise the various subtle and transcendent stations of being.

North: Gateway of the Gods
Winter Solstice: Sun door: "Exit"

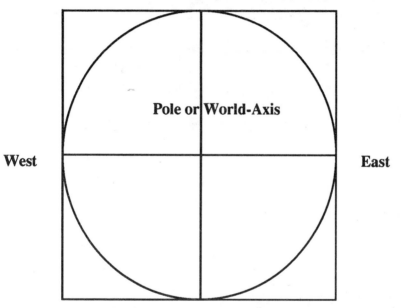

South: Door of the Ancestors
Summer Solstice
Entering the Cosmos

The Polar Axis and Spiritual Symbolism. Traditionally, in Hindu and Buddhist cosmology, north is the direction of the devayana, or 'path of the Gods'; south is the direction of the pitr-yana, or 'path of the ancestors', and of rebirth.

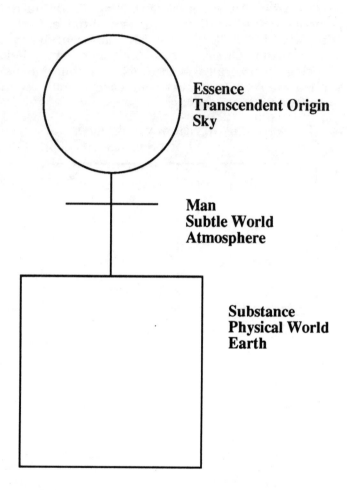

Essence
Transcendent Origin
Sky

Man
Subtle World
Atmosphere

Substance
Physical World
Earth

The Three Worlds. Above is the Transcendent, or Essence, marked by a circle; between is the subtle or psychic realm, here symbolized by the cross; and below is the physical world, here symbolized by the square. Man is mediate between above and below.

Here we see the fundamental meaning of the world-axis symbolism: the Pole round which the worlds turn is the Divine Ray of emanation, or of Creation, to use the monotheistic term, what we might call *hypodynamis*, or 'projection of energy into existence'. All the worlds are created in order (again to use monotheistic terminology) that God might reveal Himself to Himself: so the Divine emanation downwards from the Absolute Transcendent through the Angelic into the temporal, below which is the residue of creation, the hells and the sub-manifestational or chaotic, corresponds to the return journey of the individual yogi upwards through Creation, through the heavens and into absolute transcendence. Creation exists in order that man become Comprehensor, in order that man realise the Divine States, and pass beyond them into the unmanifested (*avyakta*) and then into the Supreme unmanifest (*shuddhatattva*). This is the meaning of the world-axis for man.

Hence in the Bhagavad Gita we read that 'From the realm of Brahma downwards, all worlds are subject to return to rebirth, but on reaching Me, O Son of Kunti, there is no return to birth again.'[22] He who follows the path of light Northward by way of single-minded devotion to the Highest, passes beyond the manifest and the unmanifest, or subtle realm, and enters into absolute transcendence (*parabrahman*) by virtue of this single-minded devotion, or intensity of thought, and so need not return again to the realms of suffering, of birth and death.

This devotional intensity, concentration on the Divine is known by many names: in Sufism it is reached through *dhikr*; in Hinduism it is found by means of *japa*; in Pure Land Buddhism it is entered by way of concentrating on the Divine Name (*Namu Amida Butsu*); in the Hesychastic Christian tradition it is reached by way of entry into the Jesus-prayer. But in all of these one finds the same 'rectification' of the being: thus in the *Jodo Wasan*, or Pure Land Hymns, we read:

Josan jiriki no shomyo wa,
Kasui no Chikai ni kishi te koso,
Oshie zare domo jinenni
Shinnyo no Mon ni tennyu suru.

Those who recite the Name with *joriki* (self-power)
in meditation or not,
In trusting the Vow of Ultimate Salvation
Even without being instructed, spontaneously
Turn, and enter the gate of true *bhuta-tathata*
(Thusness, or As-it-is-ness)[2] [3]

Essential here are two things: reciting the Name with
self-power (which is to say, with the power of *samadhi*, or
concentrative intensity which manifests in the *hara*, or
lower abdomen) and trusting the Vow of Ultimate
Salvation. The first — recitation — is the means; and the
second — trusting the Vow — is the orientation of the
being. Without the first, there is no intentional
'movement'; without the second, there is no proper
orientation of the being on the 'journey'. Hence both are
essential to the 'turning' and to the 'entering the gate'.

This 'turning' of the being corresponds in Christian
terms to the 'regenerated man', to the 'second birth' in
which one *recognises* one's Transcendent nature —
which is to say, turning toward the world-axis; and
'entering the gate' means passing through the 'sun-door'
in the North, or transcending all degrees of existence —
which is to say, *realising* one's Transcendent Nature.
Recitation of the Divine Names, in each of the traditions
noted, corresponds to a kind of yoga, a religious praxis
whereby one's mind is concentred on the Divine and,
even for a moment, the darkness surrounding us is
penetrated.

Admittedly this is a highly condensed description —
essentialised, one might say — whereas in more ancient
forms of yoga one finds the 'journey to the Divine' laid
out in especial detail. In the current era, which is much
'darker' and more confused than antiquity, only the
absolutely essential for liberation is emphasized. Man is
shown the way in its absolute purity: turning and

realising are underscored. Rather than following the stages which man followed in antiquity, man relies wholly on *tariki*, or 'other-power', in Christian terms, on Grace, the ineluctable complement of *joriki*, or self-power. One relies on God, not on one's own efforts.

The repetition of the *mantra* creates an 'opening' in the being whereby the Divine Grace can 'enter': rather than the practitioner following the vertical 'Divine journey' through the transcendent realms, the Divine (represented in Jodo Shinshu Buddhism by Amida Buddha descending with all his retinues at 'death', depicted in many paintings) 'descends' to man; the essential 'stages' of the ascent to liberation are condensed, as it were, in the illumination of the being.

But this in no way invalidates the symbolism of the Pole: the fact that man requires certain dispensations, a certain compensatory Divine Mercy in an era of confusion and dissolution like our own, does not mean that cosmology itself changes in any way. After all, the Pure Land Hymn we cited above still speaks of *joriki*, or self-power; it still speaks of 'turning' (in the deepest seat of one's being, as the Lankavatara Sutra has it) and it still speaks of 'entering the gate of *bhuta-tathata*, or thusness.'

I have spoken of how the recitation of the Divine Name represents a 'condensation' or 'essentialisation' of the 'journey to the Divine', if we may so speak, and hence it is important that we discuss the 'journey' in greater detail, employing the Buddhist symbolism because it represents the clearest depiction of the transmutation of consciousness. We could, for instance, turn to the 'visionary recitals' of Ibn Sina and others in the Islamic world; but in a discussion of the Pole the Buddhist symbolism of Mount Meru is perhaps more appropriate.[24]

As is evident, the symbolism of the mountain corresponds to that of the Pole: the mountain-axis is the Axis of the worlds, and hence the symbolism — once again hidden, as is the rule in Judaeo-Christian tradition

— of Moses and of Christ 'on the mountain'. Esoterically, to ascend the mountain means to ascend the world-axis, to ascend in degrees of consciousness, so to speak. Hence too the symbolism of the conical or pyramidal shape: just as consciousness is diffused below, and concentred above, so too the mountain rises, progressively, to its peak.

In the Buddhist symbolism of Mount Meru — which carries on the earlier Vedic and pre-Vedic tradition[25] — one finds precisely this axial symbolism, explicitly manifesting also the various degrees of consciousness, ranging from the *narakas* (hells) below, to the *arupaloka*, or non-form *dhyana* (absorption) above. At the base of Mount Meru one finds *akasha* (space), above which is the *vayumandala* (circle of wind), above which is the *abmandala* (circle of water), above which is the *kancanamayibhumi*, or 'golden earth'.

This 'golden earth' is the *prima materia* of Creation; it is 'that which is formed' in the cosmos, into all the worlds, and hence it is said that all the mountains of which Meru is composed are made of 'golden earth'. This is said to underscore the implications of vertical, emanatory cosmology: that which is below reflects that above. And hence, too, the 'iron wall' which surrounds Meru is not made of 'golden earth' — for its function is not reflective, but protective, holding out chaos, the infernal hordes. As the alchemical symbolism here implies, this 'golden earth', being at the 'base' of all creation, means that earth itself may be revealed as the 'pure land', or paradise — though for this, a radical transmutation of consciousness in the practitioner is necessary.

There are four 'lands' or 'realms' displayed horizontally above the realms of the 'hungry ghosts' (*pretas*) and the *narakas* (hells), these being Purvavideha in the East, Aparagodaniya in the West, Uttarakuru in the North, and Jambudvipa in the South. Of these, only Jambudvipa possesses the characteristics of the human realm — and this is only natural, South being further

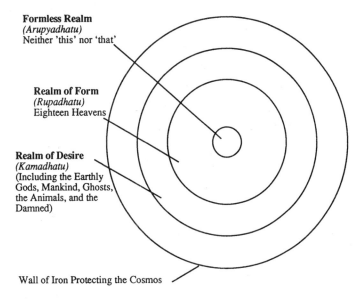

Formless Realm
(Arupyadhatu)
Neither 'this' nor 'that'

Realm of Form
(Rupadhatu)
Eighteen Heavens

Realm of Desire
(Kamadhatu)
(Including the Earthly
Gods, Mankind, Ghosts,
the Animals, and the
Damned)

Wall of Iron Protecting the Cosmos

*The Three Realms of Buddhist Cosmology. The center
(Formless Realm) is the world-axis, from where all realms of
being emanate. Hence this is also a diagram of Mount Meru,
looking directly 'down' at it. The same diagram can be
visualized as being arranged vertically, from the Formless
Realm 'above' to the humans, animals and hells 'below'.*

from the Pole and therefore subject to the vicissitudes of
birth and death, of temporal cycles. On the other hand, it
is in Jambudvipa alone that a Buddha appears (in the
waning of a cycle). This is made clearer yet by the fact
that the eight hells (four hot, four cold) are found beneath
Jambudvipa: here alone is the complete karmic cycle
possible; and only in a *saha* world, a world of suffering, is
transcendence possible. Without the impetus from
suffering, there is little incentive to attain liberation; this
is why birth in Jambudvipa is to be treasured more than
birth in one of the *devalokas*, or realms of the gods.

Above Jambudvipa are the three transcendent 'fields'
or 'realms' (though *arupyadhatu*, or the highest, formless
field, cannot be conceived as a 'realm', strictly speaking),

Realm of Non-form
i. Not Consciousness,
Not Unconsciousness
ii. No-thingness
iii. Intellectual Infinity
iv. Spatial Infinity

Realm of Form
i. Fourth Meditation
(Abodes of the Pure Ones)
ii. Third Meditation
(Beauty)
iii. Second Meditation
(Splendor)
iv. First Meditation
(Brahma)

Realm of Desire
i. Gods of Desire
ii. Mankind
iii. Ghosts
iv. Animals
v. Damned

Golden Earth
Circle of Water
Circle of Wind
Space

Buddhist Cosmology in Vertical Form. Corresponding in many respects to Platonic and Neoplatonic emanatory cosmology, here we see the Buddhist cosmology arranged vertically. In Plotinian and Platonic cosmology, one also 'ascends' from the physical realm through the transcendent realms toward the Essence, or Absolute.

and these correspond to meditational ascent through the stations of existence. To realise *arupyadhatu*, or the 'field of non-form', to pass beyond the highest of the *dhyanas* or absorptions which constitute the four 'heavens' of the *Rupadhatu*, or 'field of form', is to become an *arhat*, he who practises the *vajropamasamadhi* or *samadhi* (absorption) of the diamond throne (*vajrasana*) which is at the center of Jambudvipa (where also grows the Jambu tree for which the land is named). This latter symbolism means that at the center of Jambudvipa is the Axis of the worlds; and he who sits upon the diamond throne there (enters the adamantine concentration) transcends the cosmos entirely, attaining liberation from suffering.

Hence the Axial symbolism is here explicit: one sees the Axis of the worlds not just as the vertical connection between the various stations of being, but as the ascent from the lowest to the highest, from the *narakas* or hells, through the *manusaloka* or human realm, through the *kamadhatu*, *rupadhatu* and *arupyadhatu*, the fields of desire, of form, and of formlessness respectively; which is to say, through the realms of the gods (*kamadeva*), which include the 'four great kings' (*caturmaharajas*), the 'thirty-three heavens', the Tusita heaven, and the *nirmanarati* (gods who take pleasure in creation), and through the four *dhyanas*, or four absorptions of the *Brahmaloka*, beyond which is the interpenetrative transcendence of the *arupaloka*, or 'Formless realm'.

From this we can see how the 'fields of the Gods' (*devadhatu*) ('fields' here used in the sense of energy-field, principally) are not, in this axial symbolism, conceived as divorced from the human realm: rather, the human being may, by way of meditational absorption, enter into and realise these stations of being. The chief danger of absorption is the attractions of the bliss it proffers — one may become 'stuck' at a given station, and hence eventually 'fall'.

This is not to say, that the 'fields of the Gods' are simply psychological states, nor that they have no existence outside the individual — this sort of idea is merely modernist solipsism or egotism disguised as theorising. That the human being may realise these stations means that they exist in the same dependently originating way as human beings themselves. The Gods, strictly speaking, possess an *actually* more transcendent awareness than man, even though man possesses a *potentially* greater awareness by way of the possibility of ascending, through meditation, the Pole of being.

As Vasubhandu put it, in his *Abhidharmakosa*, the stars whirl around Mount Meru as in a whirlpool. This means that the entire cosmos, and all the stations or fields, from the most delimited below, in the hells, to the most expansive above, in the transcendent absorptions, are also *conically* arranged, hierarchically; the hells are most peripheral, and the stars, which are the visible correlates for the sempiternal 'lives' of the gods, are more central, whilst the absolute center is that of the *vajrasana*, the diamond throne upon which the yogi realises liberation, on which the arhat, the bodhisattva and the Buddha are revealed, and which is the center of the world-axis.

The world-axis is identified, throughout all the various traditions, with the cosmic Tree: in Norse tradition, for instance, it is Yggdrasil, the Tree with its roots in the underworld, its trunk and branches forming the axis of the 'nine worlds'. This triplicity, nine being three realms of three each, corresponds to the 'triple world' of earth, atmosphere and sky (*bhu, bhuvah* and *svah*) of the Hindu tradition, and together implies the complete expanse of the cosmos from the 'primordial substance' below to the realm of the Gods above.

The same symbolism holds in the Upaniṣadic tradition: in the Maitri Upaniṣad we read that the cosmic Tree's branches are 'Ether, Air, Fire, Water and Earth'; it is 'this three-fold Brahman, whose name is ''Single Fig Tree'', whose radiance is called the Sun.'[26] That the Sun, the triune Brahman, and the Single Fig Tree are synonymous is easily understood, given the symbolism we have so far elaborated: the Tree is the 'pillar' which separates earth and heaven (creating the 'three worlds'); it is the world-axis, and marks therefore the sun-door, the 'gateway' of the cosmos and the 'light of the worlds', a radiance of which the temporal Sun is but an indication.

Hence in India to this day, in the house-building ritual, one recapitulates the primordial act of Indra, the God who with his *vajra* pinned the head of the cosmic serpent Vrtra to the earth, thereby releasing the Waters of possibility which the serpent had been hindering. By hurling his *vajra* and staking the serpent's head, Indra placed in the earth the 'pillar' which separates heaven and earth, which is the axis of the Sun.[27] Thus we have here the primordial ordering and stabilising of the cosmos: in the Indian house-building ritual the mason pounds into the earth a peg which transfixes the serpent once again, for if the serpent were to get free, the cosmos would be destroyed.[28] The mason is not merely repeating Indra's transfixing the serpent; he is recapitulating the act, and the two 'fixations' are in reality one action; the mason is reinforcing the stabilisation of the cosmos.

This stabilising corresponds to other traditions as well: it will be recalled that in Genesis one finds the 'bruising of the serpent's head' after the serpent has brought about the fall of Adam and Eve.[29] Here again, the Hebrew tradition contains only a reflection of the truth, which must be extracted from it. The serpent in Genesis is, like that in the Vedas, a destabilising or disordering principle; yet without the serpent in either case, there would be no restabilising to result in the current world. This stabilising corresponds, in Scandinavian mythology, to Thor placing the world-serpent in the depths of the ocean, pinning it there until it breaks free at Ragnarok (the battle at the end of time). Indeed, the pillars of Jupiter which are found throughout Gaul and near the Rhine, put in place by the Romans, no doubt reflect and even mark the earlier pillars, the *columnae universalis* of Thor, and of the Celts.

Our point here is simple: the world-axis is, in all of these myths (with the possible exception of the myth in Genesis), divinely placed, and it 'pins down' the infernal powers below, being in essence a stabilising of the cosmos in order that the drama of existence might be played out. In Genesis, one has the Tree of Knowledge and the Tree of Life, both of which continue the axial symbolism, albeit in an implicit and attenuated way (the Tree of Knowledge is the earthly reflection of the world-axis or Cosmic Tree; and hence to choose it is to fall, as Jakob Böhme affirmed).[30]

Genesis once again can be clarified by examination of another tradition, in this case the Celtic: for just as in the Garden of Eden we see the paradisal land in which there stand sacred Trees, offering immortality, so too in Celtic myth one finds reference to *Mag Mell*, the plain of delights, to *Tir na mBec*, Land of the Living Ones, or *Tir na n-Og*, Land of the Young or Pure, and here too there are sacred Trees. In the *Rennes Dindsenchas* we find reference to five trees now fallen: 'the Tree of Ross and the Tree of Mugna, and the ancient Tree of Datha, and the branching Tree of Uisnech, and the Ancient Tree of Tortu.' Clearly these are references to ages past, to what we might call past worlds. In other places we find reference to the Land of Youth, in which death and decay is unknown, in which everywhere all is beautiful, in which the trees make music, and everywhere is gold and jewelry, the land of the Sid, to which the hero is welcomed by the goddesses there. When the Sid send a representative among men, he carries often an apple tree branch, silver with golden blossoms, able to banish pain.[3 1] The Genesis myth corresponds in some ways to the Celtic understanding of the paradisal realms 'above' the human state, realms not subject to temporal decay and relatively free of suffering.

In Genesis, it will be recalled, paradise did not cease to exist when Adam and Eve were barred from it by the flaming sword — rather, they were removed from it. But Jakob Böhme offers the inner interpretation of this myth, saying 'The Tree of Temptation was earthly, as now all Trees are; all the others were paradisiacal, from which Adam could eat paradisiacal Virtue in his Mouth.'[3 2] That is: the Tree of Knowledge is only a reflection of the Tree of Life; and when man chooses its fruit, he chooses this lower world of suffering. Hence, said Böhme, man died to Paradise, 'and got the Mind of this World, wherein sticks nothing but patching and piecing, as also Frailty, and at last Death.'[3 3]

But there is, says Böhme, a way to return to Paradise: just as man fell by choosing the Tree of Knowledge, by entering into the world of the Elements, and of suffering, so too there is a way for him to reascend to Paradise. 'Now these two Gates are in one another, the nethermost goes into the Abyss, and the uppermost goes into Paradise; and a third Gate comes to these two, out of the Element with its four Productions, and presses in together with the Fire, Air, Water and Earth, and their Kingdom is the Sun and Stars.'³ ⁴ Below this world is the Abyss; above is Paradise; and one must struggle back to Paradise, to the Virgin, who stands beyond the upward Gate and waits for man, offering him the 'Joy of the Angels, who will very kindly receive thee in thy new-born Mind and Spirit' from the 'Prison of this World'.³ ⁵

Here lies the significance of the flaming sword, according to Böhme, for 'the noble Virgin shows us the Door [and] how we must enter again into Paradise, through the Sharpness of the Sword; yet the Sword cuts the earthly Body quite away from the holy Element, and then the new Man may enter into Paradise by the Way of Life.'³ ⁶ This Sword, he continues, is the Fierceness of the Anger of God: it strips away the *spiritus mundi*, in order that regenerated man might stand in his original spiritual perfection.

By this we can see that, in the Böhmean understanding, as in the Qabalistic interpretations, the Genesis account bodies forth a traditional cosmology, albeit 'essentialised' or condensed. Rather than the elaborate cosmology even of Scholasticism, much less on the Buddhist order discussed above, we see here the essential aspects of polar cosmology: man, says Böhme, must turn away from attachment to this world, and ascend through the Gate of Life, leaving behind the earthly mind and body, receiving a new mind and body, realising his spiritual Essence, leaving behind the Four elements, and cleaving to One.

I need not here elaborate on the various paradises of the different traditions: suffice it to say that the *essential* aspects of the polar ascent, the ascent to paradise, remain the same in any case; and it is here that coincides the disparate symbolism of the Chinese 'island of the immortals' in the North, the Tibetan Northern land of Jambhala (the paradisal valley), the Celtic *Tir na n-Og*, Land of the Young or Pure, and the aboriginal shamanic belief, common in Siberian, Asian, Australian and North American shamanism, that the shaman is born in the

An Alchemical Illustration of The Great Work. In this sixteenth-century illustration we see the symbols of the alchemical transmutation. At the base of the tree is the initiate, who must die in order to live. Above, in the tree, is the initiate reborn; the figures beside the tree represent the union of above and below. Below are the opposites — sun and moon, male and female, the elements — and above is unity. This symbolism is seen in the globe held by the figure in the tree: on it is inscribed the one vertical band, below which is the realm of duality represented by the horizontal band. In this illustration too, we see the three worlds: earth, atmosphere and sky, or physical, subtle and celestial.

North, in the giant Tree that grows there.[3][7] Man can ascend the world-axis to paradise.

According to the Yakut, a Siberian tribe, incidentally, the souls of shamans are the 'knots' of the world-tree Yjyk-Mas, which reaches to the 'ninth heaven'; and as to the symbolism of 'knots' or 'coagulations', we may say that they refer to what we may call 'provisional' or 'limited' immortality, quite different from the absolute transcendence which is the result of the ascent through the 'gate of life' in the far North.[3][8] But this has to do with the limitations of shamanism in the current timecycle, with its emphasis upon the cosmological, and the absence of metaphysical principiality, which allows it to degenerate into sorcery.[3][9]

Axial symbolism, in sum, is inherent in the human psyche because it reflects the very nature of the cosmos itself. This symbolism may be hidden, or implicit within some passages within scriptures, yet so deeply embedded is the symbolism of 'up' and 'down' in the human mind that a child naturally associates heaven with 'up' and hell with 'down' as soon as the concepts are possible. Naturally, we should be careful not to 'fix' such concepts in such a way as to make of them a barrier to a deeper understanding. After all, what we call a 'meditative ascent' is not in truth an ascent at all, but we call it so because it helps us to grasp something of its nature without experiencing it directly.

So it is with all of our discussion here: obviously the only way to truly understand traditional cosmology is to experience it directly. One cannot know truly hell or heaven without living them. But, nonetheless, one ought not enter a foreign land without a map, lest one get lost and perhaps worse. If we have a general understanding, we are at least capable of grasping the general outlines of that which we might, with the help of divine grace and meditative realisation, one day see for ourselves.

The symbolism of the Pole, of the World-axis or the Cosmic Tree remains the same, paramount in all the various traditions; and without an understanding of it one cannot grasp the rest of traditional cosmology, all of which depends upon it. Without understanding that the human purpose consists in the 'ascent of the world-axis', one cannot understand the meaning of the hells and of the heavens, nor of the other realms of being, much less of the upper and lower waters, nor of subtle cosmological doctrines like that of metempsychosis; nor, for that matter, the passage from Isaiah with which we began. Upon the Axis all Creation exists, and only with this framework in mind can we pass on to the various realms and doctrines which must be understood in light of it.

Chapter III
Fire and Ice:
The Infernal States

In every tradition there is reference to sub-human or infernal stations of existence, conceived as being 'below' the human realm. Given an understanding of the cosmic Pole or Axis, we can see why this is so: the infernal states must necessarily be the furthest possible away from the Divine center; hence the hells are at once peripheral to the Axis, and are 'beneath' the realm of temporo-spatial manifestation. In Qabalistic terms, the hells are the residue or the refraction of manifestation, being at the lowest extreme of the Axis, so that beyond the infernal realms is complete chaos and dissolution. To speak of the hells is not exactly *de rigueur*, these days, but fortunately we are not constrained here by current fashions of thought.

One can easily understand why, in modernity, the infernal stations are not especially popular as a subject: their depiction, in every traditional culture, is a graphic reminder to the populace of the consequences evil has. The hells are the direct and natural consequence for certain kinds of action and intentionality. And modern man (scoffing at the popular depictions) hardly wishes to be reminded of such consequences for action and for intention.

Indeed, we need to emphasize this consequentiality here: in the modern world, surrounded by all manner of stimulation and a social environment that condones, indeed encourages, all manner of desire — that is, indeed, desire-based — it is perhaps unpleasant to find that in traditional cultures worldwide it is precisely aversion, folly and greed which are condemned as leading into the hells. But are we to believe that all mankind up to the present era was deluded, that the most diverse traditions attesting to a cosmology agreeing in its fundamentals were all in error, and that only modern man, who believes in only that which one can grasp with one's hands (as Plato put it), is wise? The reader is of course free to do so.

But for those interested in traditional doctrines it is important, first, to recognise that the *narakas* (hells) are spoken of as plural because the hells are inherently peripheral to the axis of being. Just as the heavens are naturally unitary, so too the hells must be individuated. In fact, the essence of hell is individuation, isolation of the being. Hence even though, as in Dante's *Inferno*, one may see other beings in torment, this torment only increases one's own sense of isolation, for one cannot communicate with the others; there is only one's own unceasing suffering.

There is an elaborate correspondence between the various evil acts and intentions, and their resultant manifestations in the hells. In Dante's *Inferno*, Canto XI, Vergil shows Dante Pilgrim through the seventh, eighth, and ninth circles of Hell. Vergil explains that each destructive or evil pattern in life demands a compensatory reaction in Hell. Hence 'Force on one's neighbour death and torment brings.' But the greatest sin is fraud and betrayal, and so 'in the smallest circle ... where Dis in darkness reigns, each traitor is consumed forever.'[40] Tyrants are scalded; spendthrifts are pursued by hounds; for each destructive pattern in life has its compensatory punishment. Japanese Buddhist depictions of the various punishments in the hells are also quite precise in their correspondences between deeds and results, showing disembowelments, burnings and freezings, razor-like grasses, and many other torments.

The traditional descriptions of beings in the hells are extraordinarily detailed: in the Buddhist Majjhima Nikaya we read that just as a small stone cannot compare to the mighty Himalayas, so the pain of one stabbed by three hundred spear-thrusts cannot be compared to the agony of a being in hell, so much greater is the latter. The guards of the lower worlds, we read, 'impose a fivefold punishment called the fivefold pegging: they drive a red-hot iron peg through one hand, then through the other, then through one foot and the other, and then through the centre of the chest'; or, 'having placed a man feet upwards and head downwards, they slash him with sharp knives'; or, 'the deepers of the lower worlds make that person climb up and down a great mound of burning, blazing, fiery embers'; or, 'holding him feet upwards and head downwards [they] throw him into a heated, burning, blazing and fiery iron cauldron. There he is cooked until scum bubbles up.' Or again, they throw him into an iron-walled prison, around him fire for an enormous expanse. In any of these instances, and in countless more, 'he experiences great agony, and he does not die so long as the effects of his evil keeps him there.'[41]

At first one might wonder how it is that — in Christian terms — a beneficent God would create a place of such suffering for those who do evil. However, this problem is eliminated when we step away from this specifically monotheistic view of the cosmos, and consider the hells in view of traditional cosmology more generally. That is: as we noted earlier, in view of Polar or Axial symbolism, the hells are a natural consequence of the irradiative manifestation of existence represented by the pillar or Pole of the worlds, for light must be complemented by darkness; above must be complemented by below. The hells are the residue of creation; as one moves 'down' the axis of being, one must necessarily move also 'away' from the Divine and 'outward' from the Axis. This is in fact the justification of evil's existence, evil being not just the privation of good, but its complementary antithesis, a dualism which obtains more and more starkly, the further from the Divine 'down' the Axis of being one descends.

The Torments of Hell. A medieval woodcut from Le Grande Kalendrier ... des Bergiers, Troyes, *16th century.*

But the hells are also the necessary result of human free will: the human purpose is to ascend, yet if the being's choice to live in accord with the Divine will, to ascend the Axis, to concentre himself in the Divine, is to have any meaning, there must also be a lower gate into the Abyss, just as there is a gate upward into Paradise. It is a matter of complementarity: as above, so below, but inversely. Hells inversely reflect heaven, a kind of Divine parody as it were, in which suffering replaces bliss, the King of the Dead replaces the King of Heaven, and an inverted hierarchy obtains, at the center of which is absolute solipsism (pride taken to its ultimate extent).

The hells serve a cosmic function, for in them the being is purified. Hence, 'It is said to thee, that the Wood of thy Soul shall burn in the last Fire, and that thy Soul shall remain to be Ashes in the Fire, and thy Body shall appear like black Soot.'[42] But this principle of purification has the implications of final destruction as well. In the Johannine Revelation — which details the end of the current timecycle — we read that 'This is the second death, the lake of fire; and if any one's name was not found written in the book of life, he was thrown into the lake of fire.'[43] We also read there that the Beast shall be thrown eternally into the lake of fire. This is the necessary purification of the cosmos prior to a new heaven and a new earth; for the first heaven and the first earth had passed away, and the sea was no more.[44] In order that the golden age come anew, and the current age come to an end, there must be an *apocatastasis*, a return to order: the same purification which holds on an individual basis is necessary also on a cosmic scale.

There are, then, two possibilities for beings in hell: one is that the being is purified, and enters a higher station of being once again, be it in the human or the divine realms; and the other possibility is that of complete dissolution. The 'second death' referred to in Revelation corresponds to the latter: there are beings whose essence, so to speak, is infernal wholly, or who have so completely identified themselves with the infernal as to have completely lost their transcendent essence. These, who are given sway even on earth during the 'end of the age' (and this is attested in traditional scriptures everywhere, from the Puranas, to the Sutras, to the New Testament) precede the last judgement which ends the present era, and begins the next timecycle, the golden age. For the golden age to exist upon earth, the earth must, as the *Corpus Hermeticum* has it, be purified of all evils. This is the meaning of the 'second death' and the 'closing up of hell' for all eternity. Just as for the individual to attain heaven, he must be purified of the 'residue' of his evil actions and intentions in the past, so too for the world to be renewed, there must first be purification.

This brings us to the most fundamental aspect of the hells: their nature is not different, ultimately, from that of the heavens. The same Divine Will prevails in both, but that which in heaven is perceived as delightful, in hell is perceived as agony. This truth is symbolically represented in the proto-Indo-European myth of Yama or Yima, who is the prototype ruler of the golden age and is yet king of the hells.[45] The same is represented symbolically also in the New Testament Johannine Revelation: God's face toward mankind does not change, but some men perceive the Last Judgement as God's Mercy, others as His Fierceness. In either case, however, God reveals Divine Reality in its fullness, and those whose nature is like unto Him, cleave to him. The temporal realm is ruptured; the 'shell' with which the human world currently surrounds itself is torn asunder, and the Divine Fullness is revealed in its glory, that the golden age, and the new timecycle, begins.

This means to say that the individual consists in various tendencies during life that continue after death. Thus Agrippa wrote that:

> Virgil himselfe together with the Pythagorians, and Platonists ... confesseth that separated souls retain the fresh memory of those things which they did in this life, and their will.[46]

The Last Judgement. From a Persian miniature of the 8th century.

And:

> Philosophers, think that the operations of the soul, being common to the conjoyned body, impresse upon the soul a Character of use and exercise, which it being separated will use, being strongly impressed to the like operations and passions which were not destroyed in life time. And though the body and organ be corrupted, yet the operation will not cease, but like affections and dispositions will remain. [47]

Naturally the Buddhist understanding — since it will not admit of concepts like an 'immortal soul' — would bring into question certain aspects of this observation, but nonetheless the fundamental truth it expresses corresponds to Buddhist teachings like the Yogacara concept of *alayavijnana* ('storehouse consciousness'). Briefly, we may say that the *alayavijnana* refers to the continuity of intentionality and action, so that even though there is no single being transmigrating through various existences, yet nothing is wasted. An individual's intentions and actions are 'stored' in the *alayavijnana*, and bear their fruit without fail. Hence the Buddhist, like the Christian, may say that 'though the body and organ be corrupted, yet the operation will not cease but, like affections and dispositions, will remain.'

As Agrippa points out, drawing on the Christian tradition, there are certainly instances of men 'falling into Hell' while still in the body, [48] an assertion which corresponds to similar Buddhist observations. It is often said, for instance, that those who slander the Dharma or their teacher may well fall into hell while still alive upon earth, perceiving all the torments of the afterlife before this world is yet quit. So there is a direct continuity between lives, one might say. In other words, a being whose central intentionality is discord in the religious community, will after physical death 'realise' the cosmological station and the 'being' concomitant with that intentionality — hell.

A given individual changes form not just from infancy to senility, but from instant to instant — and likewise, a being changes form again in passing from earthly existence to the hells, or to the heavenly stations. So our observations regarding Buddhist doctrines of no-self (*anatman*) must not be taken to mean that one does not suffer the consequences of one's deeds — as Christ said, one must pay the last penny. But there are more sophisticated and complete ways of understanding consequentiality and continuity. I do not speak of transmigrationism or reincarnationism, as these posit an 'immortal' being, yet we can speak of metempsychosis, of the continuity between one state of being and another.[49] In any case, for the individual in hell, it is clear he has fallen into hell.

There are certain hells in Buddhism as in Christianity (like those called Zobara and Bindara [Pindala]), from which it is said 'there is no escape', but even of these it is said only that beings in them (in the Sutra under discussion, beings who doubted Buddha's unhindered wisdom) will suffer for 'many kalpas'.[50] A kalpa is a very long time, to be sure, but it is nonetheless a duration and has its end. This end we find in the Mahaprajnaparamita Sutra, in which in a kind of celestial drama in ten acts, the Buddha enters into a *samadhirajasamadhi* (absorption in the King of Concentrations), by means of which the Buddha penetrates all ten directions simultaneously. In the successive acts the Buddha 'laughs' with his 'whole body', and beings everywhere become intent on enlightenment, so that when the Buddha enters *simhavikriditasamadhi*, or 'samadhi of the lion's play', the entire chiliocosm trembles and 'all the hells, animal births and worlds of Yama are abolished.' Those who pass from these destinies are reborn as men or Gods, and by the final act of the ten acts the entire Saha-realm, or cosmos of suffering, is transformed into a Pure Land of bejewelled transcendence.[51]

This 'cosmological' or eschatological drama corresponds to the individual transcendence of suffering: one can transpose all aspects of this macrocosmic drama to the microcosm. But the fundamental point is the same as that in certain *ahadith* in the Islamic world which read: 'Allah will save men from hell when they are burned like charcoal'; or, 'By the God in whose hands is my soul, a time shall come when the gates of hell shall be closed, and watercress (a symbol of coolness) will grown on its soil.'[52] So, be it on a macrocosmic or microcosmic scale, there must come an end to suffering. In this respect, Origen's view that all beings in hell must be saved also, though deemed heretical by certain doctors of the Church, nonetheless retains a traditional authority. Origen speaks of a 'saving pain' in temptation and suffering, saying God's 'purpose is that [sinners] may become satiated by long exposure to evil, and by being filled with the sin they desire may so perceive the harm they have taken. Then they hate what they previously welcomed; and since they have been healed more firmly, they are able to profit from the health of their souls.'[53] 'Therefore the deliverance of everyone from the Evil One must be understood in a similar way.'[54]

Likewise, Meister Eckhart says that from an ultimate perspective, time and deeds are non-existent: in the spiritual realm, that of Divine Grace, time has no place, nor does action, and neither temporality nor spatiality are admissible. Hence 'deeds and time pass away. Bad and good, they are all lost together, for they have no duration in the spirit, nor in their own right, nor have they a place of their own.'[55] As a result, 'he is blessed in whom the fruit of a good deed remains' — the spirit retains the blessing, the purification of the good deed. And again:

> when you rise above sin and turn away from it, God, who is faithful, will act as if you had never sinned at all and not for a moment will He let the former sins count against you. Even if your sins were as great in number as all mankind's put together, still he would not count them against you ... God is God of the present; as he finds a man, so he takes him and accepts him not for what he has been but for what he is now.[56]

In other words, the act of repentance, of completely turning away from attachment, aversion, and folly, of entering into what Eckhart calls 'disinterest', is inherently the transcendence of sins, a transcendence which must hold true on the cosmological as well as on the individual scale.

Since we acknowledge that, on an individual level, one may repent and purify oneself, becoming a 'new man', so too on the cosmological level there must clearly be a 'harrowing of hell', the revelation of the Divine even at the lowest reaches of the cosmos. This is symbolised in Buddhism by the presence of a Buddha — or a Buddha's hypostasis — even in the *narakas* or hells themselves.[5][7] Meister Eckhart emphasizes the non-substantiality of all causality, the illusoriness of all temporo-physical reality from the spiritual or transcendent perspective. All the evils of all mankind, from the ultimate or transcendent perspective, have no 'being' whatever, for the simple reason that evil consists in non-existence, in the absence of veracity. Thus Eckhart focuses only on the 'ennobling' of the spirit by way of the good deeds men do, this ennobling being not a transformation of the spirit but only its revelation in temporality. For there can be no debasing of the spirit, only its occlusion.

Hell, in brief, is a means of purification, the duration of suffering in it corresponding to the intensity with which a being intentionally committed evil. But this duration, like the ignorance (*avidya*) of which it is a reflection, 'is like dust which has suddenly collected on a mirror, or like clouds which have suddenly appeared in the sky', as the Hua Yen master Tzu Hsüan put it. As a result, since the root of hell itself is illusory, since the ignorance which occasions it possesses no inherent self-nature, we must admit that the hells cannot be permanent conditions.

Unless a being is completely a 'coagulation' of ignorance, composed wholly of residues (in which case it would be among that which is 'closed up forever' in the abyss, according to the New Testament), it must at heart be a manifestation of the Divine. The revelation of this essentiality is the restoration or regeneration of the cosmos, and its revelation as a Pure Land, spoken of, as we saw earlier, in the Mahaprajnaparamita Sutra, during which restoration all beings suffering in the lower realms (the hells, in particular) enter into human and divine stations.

This divine restoration is the *apocatastasis* of the Platonists and Hermetics; it is the inception of a new timecycle, the beginning of a golden age. The end of one age and the inception of the next are only causally connected — but all beings who have not attained liberation at the end of an aeon form the seeds of the beings who appear in the next *kalpa*, or timecycle. For this restoration to take place, evil must be nearly obliterated, and a shining world, in which man himself lives a near-divine existence, must manifest. There are timecycles within this larger cycle — but the same principles hold in all cases.

So hell, by its very nature, is a temporary station of being, just as are all stations within the cosmos. Not only are the stations themselves susceptible to obliteration at the end of a timecycle — and to reconstitution at the inception of the next — but each of them is 'fluid', from the perspective of individual beings. Hence, for instance, in Buddhism it is said that the Gods can fall into hell, as also beings in hell can pass into, say, the realm of the animals, or of the human. But this movement is comparatively limited in the various supra- and sub-human realms; by definition the infernal or 'lower' stations are more 'fixed', whereas the human condition is volatile, fluid.

Indeed, the human being possesses intrinsically all possible modalities of being while in this human incarnation — this being the reason that human existence is so cherished — whereas beings in the other realms are by definition more delimited, and this is true even of the Gods themselves, of whom it is said that they come to hear the preaching of enlightened human beings. As René Guénon said, 'The realisation of the total being can be attained from a basis in any one of the [possible human] states because of the equivalence of all these contingent modes of existence when regarded from the standpoint of the Absolute.'[5][8] This human life is precious for precisely this potential of transcending the limited or contingent, and realising the Absolute. The hells exist as a means of purification, and, from the religious perspective, as a 'goad' for mankind to live justly and truly, to turn 'upward' toward the Divine.

Yet the hells are only another among the many stations of manifestation possible; in the 'wheel of samsara' they are but one of the stations, or 'spokes', and from the perspective of absolute transcendence they have no more reality than any of the other stations of existence. It is true that in the monotheistic religions one finds a need to make the posthumous conditions of beings 'eternal', and this possesses a certain limited validity, insofar as existence in the hells necessarily seems indefinitely prolonged from the limited perspective of the suffering (which is itself the reason for the beings existence in the hells), and insofar as this represents a correlate to the 'eternality' of the blessed. But there is something repugnant in the opinions of those Christians who hold that the screams of the damned somehow add to the bliss of the saved. What is more, all of these opinions together are, by comparison with the vaster and more complete traditions of Buddhism and Hinduism (which maintain the interdependent relativity of all states) clearly inadequate.

For the human purpose is not merely to escape hell, but rather to completely transcend all limited, all contingent stations. And with this, we conclude our discussion of the hells themselves, moving on, briefly, to consideration of the other sub-human or extra-human realms of the cosmos.

Chapter IV
Infrahuman and Extrahuman Stations

Although I spoke first of the *narakas* (hells), these stations form only a part of the infrahuman stations possible, and these in turn are only a portion of the cosmological conditions or levels 'beneath' the human station. I discussed the hells first because, from the human perspective, they form the most important of the various infrahuman conditions possible, representing as they do either a purificatory or a retributive station, depending on whether one views them from the metempsychosic or the monotheistic point of view. But for a more complete understanding, let us step back from purely human considerations — though we cannot leave that perspective entirely — and consider the subhuman aspects of the cosmic axis more generally.

In the first chapter of Genesis we read the following: 'And God said: "Let there be a firmament in the midst of the waters, and let it separate the waters from the waters." And God made the firmament and separated the waters which were under the firmament from the waters which were above the firmament.'[5 9] As they stand, the verses cannot be interpreted in any literalist manner: what on earth can this mean, this separation of the waters above from the waters below?

By way of Hindu doctrines we can see what is meant here: the Waters are, respectively, the Upper and the Lower Waters, the Earth (*prthivi*) being the 'condensed' or 'congealed' foam (in the phrase of the Brhadaranyaka

Upaniṣad) of the Lower Waters, which are the 'ocean of infinite possibility'.[60] In other words, the Lower Waters are like a mirror, upon which the various reflective possibilities of the Divine in existence play. The Upper Waters are unmanifested possibility, corresponding in some aspects to the Platonic 'realm of ideas'.[61] Or again, the Upper Waters are Essence, and the Lower Waters are the Substance in which it manifests.

This human life is a voyaging between these two. Says Coomaraswamy:

> The Waters and the Earth are to be understood not only with reference to our terrestrial seas and continents, but as respectively the possibilities of existence in any of the Three Worlds, and the support of living beings existent in any one of them according to the terms of its possibilities: in other words, the "Waters" are literally *peut être, bhavisya*, the Earth [or] any corresponding plane or sphere (*loka, dhatu, ksetra, bhumi*) or support (*pratistha*) of experience: and any such Earth floats like a lotus, or like foam, or like a ship, on the surface of the Waters.[62]

Man exists as the median point between the 'two oceans': his realm is that in which essence, or formless possibility (*purusha*) meets formal possibility, or substance (*prakriti*), and these are symbolised by the circle of heaven and the square of the primordial substance, the *prima materia* of the cosmos. These two — essence and substance, or 'light of heaven' and 'light of nature' — form the two poles of the cosmos, above and below, and from this we can understand that that above is reflected in that below, that the light of nature is a reflection in the primordial waters of possibility, of the Upper Waters of nonmanifestation. Above, then, is the sphere, and below the cube; above is the perfection of the cosmic egg, and below the extension into manifestation of the square into the cube, all of these forms having correspondent representation in the Buddhist symbolism of the stupa.[63]

So, 'beneath' the square of primordial substance, which is the reflection of the Divine Plenipotentiality above, is the chaos of indefinitude. The irradiation of the

Divine, even in its reflection in nature, acts as a wall or barrier against the chaos which lies 'without' the cosmos. No human being can enter into chaos, by definition. This chaos below nature is the Abyss of which Böhme speaks, and it is the abolition of individuality in the swarming aimlessness of the disordered, the 'unformed'. As such, it is the inversion of the selflessness found in heaven. In heaven, one enters into the transmutation of individualisation, this being the bliss of heaven; entering the chaos below, one enters into the dissolution of the self. This dissolution, incidentally, is the 'function' of various pseudo-religious cults of the current day, which rather than leading mankind upward toward the Divine, drag it downward into the abyss.[64] But on this we need not dwell here.

Naturally, there is an indefinitude of other 'stations' which do not correspond exactly to the human mediate position, stations of being which are removed from the Axis in various degrees and which for the individual human-being represent sub-human or extra-human states: they lack the axiality, or the centrality which characterises the human possibilities. Among these certainly we may count the 'hungry ghosts' or *pretas* of Buddhist tradition, the *asuras* of Vedic and Buddhist tradition, the *jinn* of Islamic tradition and the faery of Celtic tradition, as well as the giants, dwarves, elves and other beings of various cultures, beings now supposed to be mythological. Of course, I am by no means suggesting that these various beings are all equivalent — far from it. I am rather here saying that they each, as various classes, kinds or species, all correspond to extrahuman stations of being: they do possess stations on the cosmic axis, but are 'further' from the axis, from centrality, than the human station, and only under certain conditions[65] are in direct communication with the human being, who alone among beings conjoins circle and square, heaven and earth, above and below, at least potentially if not actually, by way of spiritual realisation.

Of course, extrahuman beings may also attain some

degree of spiritual realisation: in the Koran, for instance, in the *sura al-Jinn*, we read of the *jinn* that 'Some of us are righteous, while others are not; we follow different ways.' 'We have heard a wondrous discourse giving guidance to the right path. We believed in it, and henceforth shall serve none besides our Lord.'[66] That the *jinn* correspond to the *asuras*, or giants, we find by the ensuing statement: 'We made our way to high heaven, and found it filled with mighty wardens and fiery comets. We sat eavesdropping, but eavesdroppers find flaming darts in wait for them. We cannot tell if this bodes ill to those on earth, or if their Lord intends to guide them.'[67] The *jinn*, here, correspond to the 'watchers' in the *Book of Enoch*: they are the Fallen Angels, some of whom shall realise spiritual regeneration, others of whom will not, rather dissolving in the abyss.

I will not here elaborate the variations between all the beings, as recognised by the various traditional cultures, nor will I consider all the possible extrahuman and subhuman stations, for that would take far too much space. Rather, I shall consider each of the classes or kinds of being by *genera*, and in this more systematic way delineate the general outlines of extrahuman and subhuman possibilities, reference to which is still preserved in the various traditions.

To begin, we may turn to Ko Hung, a fourth-century Chinese alchemist who transmitted to posterity directions for entering the mountains, directions which chiefly consisted in ways of recognising the elemental or subtle beings who might harm one who was unprotected. Hence he says:

> If you should see there at night an alien [*hu*], it will be the power in copper and iron; if it looks like a man from Ch'in, it will be the power from a one-hundred-year-old tree. ... If you should see an official in a mountain stream his name will be Ssu-chiao. Shout that name, and everything will be well. Proceed likewise, should you meet in the mountains with a large snake wearing a turban, its name being Sheng-ch'ing.[68]

Ko Hung goes on to elaborate the particular days (particular astrological rulerships) on which these various beings might be able to penetrate the temporo-physical realm and even cause harm to humans. The primary way of avoiding harm is to know the creature's name; to see it and to know its name and nature is to control it.[69]

Some of these are the elemental spirits, being connected with the various kingdoms of earth, water, fire, wood and metal, and of them Agrippa says, in the West:

> There is moreover as hath been above said, a certain kind of spirits not so noxious [as hagges], but most neer to men, so that they are even affected with humane passions, and many of these delight in man's society, and willingly dwell with them: Some of them dote upon women, some upon children, some are delighted in the company of divers domestic and wild animals, some inhabit Woods and Parks, some dwell about fountains and meadows. So the fairies, and hobgoblins inhabit Champian fields; the Naiades fountains; the Potamides Rivers; the Nymphs marshes, and ponds; the Oreades mountains; the Humedes Meadows; the Dryades and Hamadryades the Woods, which also Satyrs and Sylvani inhabit, the same also take delight in trees and brakes, as do the Naptae, and Agaptae in Flowers; the Dodone in Acorns; the Paleae and Feniliae in fodder and the Country.[70]

Hence:

> The bonds by which spirits are bound, besought, or cast out, are three; some of them are taken from the elemental world, as when we adjure a spirit by any inferior and natural things of affinity with or adverse to them, ... as by flowers and herbs, by animals, by snow, by ice, by hell, by fire, and such like ... The second bond is taken from the Celestial world, viz, when we adjure them by the heaven, by Stars ... The third bond is from the Intellectual and divine world, which is perfected by religion ... wherefore this bond is the highest of all and the strongest.[71]

This kind of hierarchy holds in both the Orient and the Occident. In the Chinese thaumaturgy, the subtle world is conceived, like the human, in terms of ranks and hierarchies. This is why Ko Hung refers to the various beings one might encounter in the mountains as 'ministers', or as 'officials' in the streams, the trees, and so forth. These elemental beings are, in the cases to which Ko Hung refers, often intent upon deluding or misleading man, leading him to his destruction but, says Agrippa, they are so primarily to 'noxious men', for 'they are afraid of and flie from men of a constant, bold and undaunted mind, being in no way offensive to good and pure men, but to wicked and impure, noxious.'[7 2]

In Japanese tradition, as in the Greek, one often finds reference to men who, after death, became 'mountain spirits', often because of foul play, because they desired revenge from something done against them or the like. One can easily understand why this is so by considering that a single-minded desire for revenge, say, at the moment of death is rather like a 'deflection' of the being. Rather than being oriented toward the cosmic Axis, toward a heavenly station, the being's energy is oriented 'horizontally', toward earthly revenge, and this single-minded, albeit misdirected energy causes what the Greeks call *cacodaemons*, or evil spirits, as well as 'hags and hobgoblins' in European tradition, just as a single-minded intention to, say, save beings in the mountains is an 'horizontalised' energy which creates *eudemons*, or blessed spirits. All of these beings, then, are peripheral to the human realm, many being in one way or another 'residue' of human intentionalities and desires 'deflected' or 'reflected' from an orientation toward the Divine.

But not all beings are residue of the human realm. Certainly ghosts, hobgoblins, hags, and *pretas* (hungry ghosts) in the Buddhist tradition can be so classed. However, there are also beings whose central principle is not of light, but rather of darkness and wrath. Of these Jakob Böhme writes:

> There is no pain in the creatures which have been created in the dark world; for they are of the fierce wrathful property, and know nothing of the light. Fierceness is their strength and might, and enmity their

will and life. The more evil and hostile a creature is in the dark world, the greater its might. As the powerful tyrants of this world often exhibit their power in malignity, so that men must fear them, or as tame animals are afraid of ferocious ones; so has this likewise a property in the dark world.[7 3]

This 'dark world' in some ways corresponds to the human, for 'what all wicked men in this world do in their malice and falsehood, that also ... the other creatures do in the dark world.'[7 4] Man may choose whether to live under the dominion of the 'world of light' or under that of the 'dark world', for though he was created for the first, yet he chose to awaken the second, the dark world, and now must combat it, that he may live in his native spirit of love again.[7 5]

But there are creatures in the dark world which do not correspond to the human realm, though because their principle is wrath and anguish they will take advantage of the human if an opening is presented. We speak here in part of the hells, when speaking of the dark world, but strictly speaking the hells are directly referential to the human condition, and to the evil that men do; whereas the dark world refers to the infernal and subhuman realms generally, whence Böhme's reference to the 'other creatures' there. Because of human centrality the dark world will seize upon any opening to enter the human realm and 'drag down' man into their ranks, and as the protective sphere which inherited religious tradition afforded mankind erodes and cracks ever more in the current *kali yuga*, the 'final age' of the current timecycle, these beings are given ever more opportunity to infiltrate themselves into the human realm and wreak destruction.

These beings are not the 'residue' of human intentionality as are, say, ghosts or other peripheral beings hovering on the fringes of human life. Rather, they are the residue or 'shell' of creation itself, to which the Qabala refers as *qlipoth*, or the 'rinds' of creation. That is, in the process of Divine emanation, or Creation, the Divine power when it enters a primordial substance — a world if we may so speak (a matrix of creation) — it necessarily 'spills over': for manifestation is necessarily the meeting of two disparate and incommensurate powers, one the primordial substance (*prima materia*), the central quality of which is resistance and malleability; the other the Divine emanation, which forms and informs, enlivens, empowers. Their relation to the human world is simply this: that the 'dark powers' must continually strive to usurp the 'powers of light', and as the human realm is central, stretching into both, the human becomes a realm of combat.

So we may speak of the following *genera* of subhuman and extrahuman realms: first, there are the extrahuman beings like the *asuras*, about whom we shall speak at much greater length shortly. Then there are the subhuman stations like the elementals, who are the forces inherent in Creation itself, the subtle beings of fire, air, earth and water, metal and wood, the naiads, dryads, and so forth of whom Agrippa spoke. And there are the peripheral stations like those of the ghosts and *pretas*, the goblins and hags, the beings who bear a direct relation to the human realm, being an 'outgrowth' of it, a kind of 'horizontalising' of human aspirations toward the divine, often the result of violence, of revenge, of anything which creates a single-minded intentionality. (The beings of whom Ko Hung spoke are an admixture of these two realms.) Finally there are the denizens of the 'dark world', of whom Jakob Böhme spoke: these consist in wrath and destruction principally, and though they are not a 'result' of the human intentionality, they would fain ever enter the human realm in order to continually attack, by way of it, the powers of light against which they continually struggle.[7][6]

Thus we can see that although the human realm is not necessarily the cause of the elemental or infernal powers (the former being manifestation of the Divine creative power, the second being its 'residue'), it is central to all of them: the human, by virtue of his axiality, is essential to all the beings, subhuman, extrahuman alike; it is in the human realm that the 'battles on the field of manifestation' take place. The nature of these battles — in particular those involving the *asuras* — are the subject of our next section, and to them we now turn.

Chapter V
Titans and Men:
Catastrophe and Wisdom

Henry Corbin once wrote that the traditional view of man presents a direct contrast to that held by the merely human sciences. According to Corbin:

> Present mankind is regarded [traditionally] not as a summit of progress but as descended from a superior mankind through a catastrophe of whose mystery we can gain only a distant intimation ... In short, there was a race of beings superior to ours, who were the educators of our race; to this race belonged the Adam of the Bible and Koran. Far from having been the first man on earth, Adam was one of the last survivors of the cycle of Epiphany preceding our own cycle of Occultation. [7 7]

We need not dwell here upon Adam, but we ought to make mention of the Biblical passages after the story of Adam, Eve, and the Garden: for after Adam and Eve have had children, and after Cain in fact had been marked by God as the wanderer, he was said to have gone out and *built a city*. Now how could he have built a city, had Adam, Eve and their children been the only beings on earth? In answering this question we will come to understand the nature of the Titans, and of our own era.

Clearly the Biblical version of history is an attenuated one, a fact to which we have alluded before. As Martin Lings has pointed out, one finds in the Judaeo-Christian perspective a limitation to a single timecycle, and hence one finds logical dissonance in certain of the references, dissonance which can only be explained by comparison with, say, Buddhist or Hindu teachings regarding the vaster timecycles within which the Judaeo-Christian view takes but one.[7][8] That it is possible for the Judaeo-Christian or Islamic perspective to embrace the wider view is proven by the existence of the Qabalistic teachings in Judaism, and by the Isma'ili teachings in Islam, both of which contain essentially Oriental doctrines, with which an esoteric amplification of the scriptures is possible, indeed demanded, for a complete understanding of their meaning.

So, to continue the question we posed earlier: how is it that there were cities — how could Cain build a city — with only his own family populating the earth? Obviously he could not do so: there had to be many human beings, or beings, populating the earth, but Genesis focuses on the history of one lineage. Yet then the question naturally arises: what sort of a population was there at the time of Adam and Cain? That the population was not merely human is indicated in Genesis 6:4, in which one finds reference to the sons of God marrying the 'daughters of men', as well as to a race of giants upon the earth. Immediately after this passage, we find reference to Noah, to the story of the Flood and of the ark; so we know that there is a connection between the Flood, which wiped out a corrupt race, and the giants or Titans.

The Old Testament gives us only the barest hints and glimpses of these primeval connections, of this mythological prehistory of the world, and so in order to understand more clearly the nature of these events which took place on the 'border of time', so to speak, in the timecycle before our own, separated from us by cataclysms greater than we can imagine, we must turn to the histories preserved in other scriptures and mythological traditions: we must turn to the Eddas, to the Voluspa, to the Teutonic myths and to the Mahabharata and the Vedas, to the Buddhist Sutras and to Isma'ili teachings. For by means of these, we can begin to discern what happened in that 'time before our time', begin to understand those events the shadows of which still touch us now.

To begin, we must clarify our interpretation of the words 'Fallen Angel', 'Titan', *asura* and the like. I take these terms to be roughly equivalent, recognising that there are cultural differences in their meaning, but nonetheless asserting that these cultural differences entail different perspectives of the same events, the same cataclysms, and the same beings. We discern the outlines of a proto-religious understanding underlying all the various traditions we now possess. For our aim here is not merely discussion of this or that tradition, creating a sort of grab-bag of myths for the reader, but rather, I wish to treat — as do the various religious traditions — the myths in question as pointing to cosmological truths, events which have a direct and an indirect bearing on our own lives.

When we turn to the well-known 'sixteen hymns' of Rg Veda X.90 (*purusasukta*) we find that the cosmos was created by the primordial sacrifice of the *purusa*, the primordial Giant, the sixteen parts beginning with the feet and knees, ending with the skull, these corresponding to the cosmos itself. The winds in the cosmos correspond to the primordial *prana*, the breath of the giant.[79] Of course 'cosmic wind' or *prana* has as pivotal a function in the cosmos as it does in the individual: the cosmic wind carries seeds of the dissolved Creation through to a new birth, to new worlds and the onset of a new timecycle.[80]

But this fundamental sacrifice, the sacrifice (*yajna*) which lies at the center of the cosmos itself, at its creation, has its reverberations throughout the ensuing timecycles which that sacrifice of the giant inaugurates. Obviously, if the very inception of the cycle is the conversion of a Titanic power to a more stable, protecting power, then this same scenario must necessarily be repeated throughout all subsequent cycles: and so in fact we find it. Indeed, this is the key to all the various myths of the Titans and their subjugation to the later powers of the Gods: it is not that the Titans are necessarily superior

Giant and Dwarves

beings, but they are a great power, which must be tamed in order that the cosmos remain in balance: untamed power must be tamed so it does not run amok. But more of this in a moment.

In a sense, the *mahapurusa* can be identified with the *danavas*, or *asuras*, the Titanic beings mentioned throughout the Puranas and Vedas. For in fact, just as the primordial sacrifice of the giant 'precedes' or 'is' creation of the cosmos, so too the *danavas*, and indeed the *asuras* as a whole, 'precede' the appearance of the Gods themselves in the cosmos. There is also a tradition which holds that Yama, Lord of Death, is the progenitor of mankind, in concert with his brother Manu the lawgiver. In this view, Yama corresponds to the Iranian Yima, first man and first king of mankind, *yamana* meaning 'restrainer'. And additionally, Yama was the 'first sacrifice'.

By homologisation with the primordial sacrifice that is existence, man is capable, by 'projection' (*nyasa*), of realising his nature as microcosm, of realising unity with the cosmos as a whole, and with the Gods, who after all proceeded from the sacrifice of the primordial giant.[81] This unity manifests in meters, the feet (*padam*) of the sacred verses corresponding simultaneously to aspects of the primordial man, and to the fundamental structure of the cosmos. Just as the Gods proceeded from that primordial sacrifice, so too everything in creation bespeaks it. The very earth itself is in a profound way consanguine with the giants, or Titans as a race.

Sacrifice is invariably — in a religious context — a transmutation of a lower to a higher power. This is so whether in an animal sacrifice, or in the wider context of the subjugation of an entire race of beings or religious understanding to another. When Buddhism entered Tibet, for instance, there were many fierce deities from the native Bön-po religion, all of whom were subdued and brought into the fold of Buddhism by the meditative power of Padma-Sambhava, making them protective deities under the new tradition, so that there is a direct continuity between the two religious cycles. In such a subordination of the earlier to the later tradition, there is at times an attenuation of the truth.

Time after time historically, one finds reminders of the subjugation of primal powers and the restoration of order: what we call 'history' is, after all, a series of reflections, reflections of primordial cosmic events. Hence I am not among those who hold that the subordination of the *danavas* or *asuras* by the Gods referred to in the Vedas and Puranas is merely a mythologem for the triumph of some ancient warrior tribe over another. Myths are not merely literary ways of telling history: rather, history is a prosaic way of manifesting the eternal truths expressed in myth. In the case of the *asuras*, we find that this is precisely the case: the battle of the *asuras* and the Gods is not a mythologising of some historical battle; rather, the *asuras* and the Gods are principles which manifest throughout human history.

The myths surrounding the *asuras* and the *devas* are of profound interest, for they demonstrate precisely this principle. The *asuras* were originally, in the earliest Vedas, not regarded as demons but rather as Gods themselves, or in any case as a race of pious, essentially good beings. Indeed, the word 'asura' was used to signify Indra, Varuna and other Gods, and corresponded with the Ahura-Mazd of the Zoroastrian tradition; it derived from *as* (to breathe), and the connections with *prana* or 'vital life force' are evident. What is more, the *asuras* were recognised as a race of wise beings, virtuous, good, charitable, and full of deep knowledge.

Indeed, Sri, the Goddess of beauty and fortune, dwelt with them in an earlier timecycle, and in particular with the *danavas*, or giants.[8][2] But after a time the *danavas* became proud and overbearing, destroying their previous harmony with the earth. As the Mahabharata has it, in a much earlier and purer timecycle, nearer the Golden Age, men lived in harmony with one another and with their world. Their offspring lived for hundreds of thousands of years, free from worry and disease, living in accord with the Law, kings protecting their subjects, all creatures flourishing upon the earth, without vice among men.[83]

But then the *daityas* (*genii*) and *danavas* took birth among men, and bloated with pride, insolent, they swarmed over the earth, ignoring the four-caste system, destroying the homes of men and the peaceful way of life, slaughtering everywhere, laying waste to the earth until finally Earth herself had to plead with Brahma to make this disruption end.

Brahma then decreed that the Gods, the *gandharvas*, and the *apsaras* be born among men, at least a 'part of themselves', in order to throw off earth's burden. Thus 'the celestials in succession descended from heaven to earth, for the destruction of the Gods' enemies, and the well-being of all the worlds; whereupon they were born in the lineages of *brahmins* and of *ksatriyas* (priests and warriors), slaying the *raksasas*, the *danavas*, the *gandharvas* and the *nagas* in great profusion.'[84] So with the descent of the Gods, order was restored: the *asuras*' destruction was halted.

Yet there are many questions which remain regarding this rather simplified and, at first, confusing account. For instance: why is there such fluidity among sides? According to this account the *gandharvas*, for instance, are said to slay *gandharvas*; and the *nagas* and *raksas* are only mentioned later on, so one is not precisely sure who is on which side, save that the primary conflict was between *asuras* and *devas*, or the Fallen Angels and the Angels. In fact this conflict is the organising principle: the fates of the other kinds of beings are determined by their relation to these central two classes. These two classes, in turn, are known by relation to the human realm, in which they manifest. For man possesses a fluidity of being whereby Gods, *asuras*, and other kinds of beings may all enter into the human station in this less solidified, 'earlier' timecycle preceding our own.

But other questions remain: why, for example, do we read that the *asuras* are here wholly destructive, when in the Rg Veda *asuras* is synonymous with Gods? In part, the answer no doubt has to do with the fluidity to which we made reference before: some beings identify with destructive power, some with creative. Later in the Mahabharata, after all, we read of the *asura* Nikumbha, whose two sons made a vow to conquer the universe. These twins were consecrated, went forth, and performed such awesome austerities that even the Gods became frightened at their self-mortification, for with it came enormous powers. The Gods sent them all manner of illusions in order to tempt them away from the austerities, but finally they attained their goal, the King of the Worlds coming to grant them a boon. They requested magical power, weapon-power, strength and immortality (the traditional attributes, save for immortality, of the Titans in all antiquity). 'You may have all but immortality,' said the King. 'Then let us be vulnerable only to one another,' said the twins. 'So shall it be,' said the Grandfather of all being. And so the twins consciously decided to embody destructive power: they laid waste to all the world, finally disporting themselves with all jewels and drink and women wherever they liked, atop mountains and in valleys, satiated until the Grandfather of the worlds sent Tilottama, a magnificently beautiful woman, to tempt them. Then the two twins fought among themselves over her and killed one another, whereupon their armies of *asuras* fled with their women back into the underground world whence they had arisen.[8][5]

Here we see again the *asuras* identified with destructive power by conscious choice: not all *asuras* participated. This insurrection of *asuras* against the Gods must have taken place after the Gods had driven them into their underground or sub-terrene (to be more precise) cities ages before, for it is said that the *asuras returned* to their sub-terrene existence. Their rebellion was put down not by sheer force, but by subterfuge, indicating that this was not a war, but a later insurrection after the war had been won.

In any event, to return to the question with which we

prefaced this myth: how are the *asuras* identified at one time with good, and at later times with evil? Shankaracarya, in his commentary on the Chandogya Upaniṣad, goes so far as to equate the *asuras* wholly with the worldly powers that inhibit spiritual development: the *asuras* are that which holds man back from ascent to the Divine knowledge, he says.[8][6] Though this interpretation is wholly valid for practical purposes (from the perspective of spiritual praxis) it eliminates many subtle aspects of the *asuras*' nature which we must here examine in order to fully understand their essence and relation to man and to the present age.

For though one can allegorize the conflict of the *asuras* and the Gods, making of it an internal religious conflict within the ascetic, this interpretation ignores the ways that this conflict reappears throughout the world's traditions, and most importantly, it ignores the cosmological aspects of that conflict, both in terms of the sons of Elohim 'marrying the daughters of men', and in higher terms, the Antigods' cosmological significance in explaining the true nature of evil. Allegorizing is practical in that it relates every religious or mythological being or image to the individual; but we need not be limited to that. To discuss these things in depth, we must begin to separate them out, focusing upon different aspects of the Titanic myths, beginning first with the generation of giants and men, moving then to the more transcendent implications of the struggle between Gods and Antigods, between the Gods and the Titans.

I alluded earlier to the mating of giants and of men; but before we discuss this, let us cite the order of creation according to the Norse Edda, in particular the Gylfaginning, or 'Beguiling of Gylfi', in which we read the following by the King Gylfi, who called himself Gangleri,[8][7] and who questioned the three rulers he encountered on a magical journey to Asgard as follows. Gangleri asked: 'Who is foremost or oldest, of all the Gods?'. Harr (the highest King) replied: 'He is called in our speech Allfather, but in the Elder Asgard he has twelve names ...'. Then Jafnharr spoke (the second king) and then the third, who spoke of Allfather's creating the spirit, that good men go up to Gimle, or heaven, evil men down to misty Hel, the ninth world. Then asked Gangleri: 'What did Allfather before heaven and earth were made?'. Answered Harr: 'He was then with the Rime-giants.'

The Rime-giants, in other words, preceded human beings of the present timecycle; they were created of the venom or 'rime' which emerged from the meeting of the primal heat of the volcano, and the ice. First created was Ymir (semantically correlate to Yama), from whom the other giants appeared by spontaneous generation from his body (from his left hand and his feet, generated out of his venomous sweat). More were created later, by the licking of the great cow named Audumla on salt blocks. The sons of Borr, one of these first generations of giants (the issue of a marriage between giants) then slew Ymir, and of his body was the earth created. Of his blood came the sea, of his skull was heaven made, of his bones and flesh was made the earth. And when Ymir was slain, the waters-blood flowed so freely, that all the Rime-giants but one were drowned, that one being Bergelmir, who lived in a ship with his wife.

This corresponds very much to the tale of Noah: and indeed, both here in the Eddas and in Genesis we find ancient memories of a catastrophe which ended the timecycle prior to our own. The sketchiness of the Eddas' description is no doubt because there is a kind of barrier between one cycle and the next, so that only intimations of the last cycle are possible for man in the next. Indeed, the view seen in the Eddas is by no means complete: it is rather a condensed vision, in which we see primordial Creation, then the ending of the cycle immediately previous to our own. In the Voluspa, which recalls a greater antiquity, and hence a wider purview, we read:

Gathered the Gods on the Fields of Labour;
They set on high their courts and temples;
They founded forges, wrought rich treasures ...
They played at tables in court, were joyous —

Little they wanted for wealth of gold —
Till there came forth three of the giant race,
all fearful maidens from Jötunheim.
Then went all the Powers to their thrones of doom.[8 8]

Here we find reference to the golden age; but just as in
the Mahabharata and the Vishnu Purana, the golden age
is brought to a close by the arising of the Titans, who
bring about a great battle between the Gods and the
giants. I already spoke of how, in the Mahabharata, the
giants and Gods took birth among men and battled until
the Gods were victorious (at least for a time); here we
have the same scenario.

In the Voluspa, after the passage quoted, we find long
lineages of giants, this corresponding to the lineages of
the Mahabharata, in which we also see an intertwining of
the giants and the humans. And after this we find the
line:

I remember the first great war in the world.[8 9]

But this passage — referring to the first battle between
Gods and Antigods — nearly blurs into the final
discussion of the last battle, Ragnarok, the battle at the
end of time; and this is not surprising, for the various
'wars' are in fact reflections, manifestations of the primal
metaphysical drama of which we shall shortly speak.
From a metaphysical perspective, after all, the various
cosmological events are merely reflections; and from that
perspective, 'time' is of no consequence. First and last are
one.

So again: to speak of the intermarriage of giants and
men — or of Gods and men — is not merely a figure of
speech, an allegorical way of expression. Rather, it is
clear from Norse and from Vedic and pre-Vedic writings,
as from Genesis, that a race of giants preceded man on
earth; and that the previous timecycle ended in a
cataclysm, from which only a few survived, those
intermarrying with mankind, passing on also the secrets
of magic and of primordial wisdom; for they are the
keepers of the ancient wisdom, the sciences of the earth.

This is not to say that the giants no longer exist, only that they do not exist on this present earth: legend after legend speaks of their confinement to other worlds and cities of their own, of their enchainment in order that they not disturb the world's order once again.

That contact with the cities of the *asuras* and other like beings is possible in the present era can be seen by the fact that Nagarjuna, the 'second Buddha', found the teachings he revealed in the keeping of the *nagas*, serpentine beings to whom the Buddha had entrusted that wisdom which was efficacious for liberation in the midst of this, the *kali yuga*, or dark age. In this instance, the *nagas* were beneficent beings; but the serpentine demons are not always so: indeed, the struggle related in the Vishnu Purana between Krishna and Kaliya, the demonic serpent that had oppressed an entire area, corresponds to other struggles between heroes and demons — one thinks of Beowulf — and in fact correlates to the primordial struggle between Vishnu and the primordial serpent of chaos. The hero represents the power of ordering; the demon is chaos, the primal night, the *pralaya*, that which lies between the timecycles.

This brings us back to the metaphysical aspects of the struggle between the giants or *asuras*, and the Gods. As is repeated throughout the Norse myths, the Gods are forever engaged in the binding of the dark powers — just as in the Hindu mythology, the Gods are struggling against the *asuras* to maintain order. And in Scandinavian mythology this struggle was essentially a magical binding, the weaving of magical knots to hold back the powers of darkness: Tyr bound Fenris the wolf, Thor bound the serpent and cast it into the sea, and Loki was bound by the Gods until Ragnarok and the end of time. These events are inscribed in jewelry and elsewhere, not to commemorate, but to seal and to participate in that binding: hence knots and intricate bindings play a central role in Scandinavian 'decoration'. All of these bindings repeat the primordial binding which placed the serpent 'Fierce-stinger' at the base of

Yggdrasil, the world-tree; they manifest, indeed, the ordering of the cosmos itself.

But the giants are not precisely 'dark powers'; rather, they are ambivalent beings, at times the teachers of the Gods, so that even Odin had to go to the Titans for counsel, as Indra and the other Vedic Gods went to the *asuras* for the *amrita* and for knowledge. Indeed, Mimir, a water giant, was the teacher of Odin and the other Norse Gods, though a Jötun; from Mimir came Odin's 'wisdom of wands' and magic rings, the ability to see far into distant worlds.[90] Yet in Voluspa we read also:

> Far east in Ironwood sat an ancient giantess
> Fenrir's offspring she fostered there
> From them all doth one come forth
> In guise of a troll, to snatch the sun.
>
> He is gorged as on lives of dying men;
> he reddens the place of the Powers like blood.[91]

This myth repeats in Norse form that which appears also in the Mahabharata and the Puranas, to which we have already made reference. Just as Rahu, the 'seizer of the Sun', was a giant (*danava*) who sought to drink the nectar of immortality (*amrita*), but who was caught by the Gods as he drank, beheaded, and his head then perpetually sought to devour the Sun and Moon, so too in Norse tradition, Sköll the wolf and his companion seek to destroy the Sun and Moon; and they are kin of Fenris, the wolf who seeks to destroy all the world. They are spoken of in Grimnismal, just before Grimnir, or Odin, says:

> They called me sage and wise when I duped
> the old Jötun dwelling beneath the earth
> and slew single-handed the son
> of that monster who owned the mead.
>
> They call me now Odin, but erewhile the Dread one
> Thund was I called before that.[92]

Clearly Odin's journey to the world of the giants, one of the three roots of Yggdrasil, the world-tree, resulted in a change of state: he became Odin because he had attained the Song-mead. But at the same time, destructive power in the form of the giant's kin Fenris and Sköll also proceeds from the giant-world.

Again we can see the ambiguity of the Titanic position: on the one hand holders of wisdom which even the Gods envy, on the other hand the Titans are the source of destructive power. In brief, the Titans manifest the same kinds of ambiguity as do human beings themselves. We shall see this very relationship clarified by considering the metaphysical implications of the Titanic powers.

Henry Corbin, in his work on Isma'ili gnosis and its connections with the Iranian mythos of Ahura-Mazd and Ahriman (which translates into, in Islamic terms, the heavenly Adam and Iblis, and in Judaic terms, the Angel and Azaziel), alluded to the metaphysical implications which are reflected in the battle between the *devas* and the *asuras* in Indian tradition, and between the Angels and the Fallen Angels in the Judaeo-Christian-Islamic traditions. In all these names mentioned above, one sees the same trans-temporal conflict manifesting, which Corbin delineates as follows:

> It 'happened' that in a vertiginous stupor the spiritual Adam — the Third Angel, whose innermost being concealed the Azaziel-Iblis (the other protagonist of this drama in the *Umm al-Kitab*) — brought this [the emanation of the Divine] to a halt. Like Azaziel, he agreed to recognise the *Mubdi*, but he refused to recognise the pre-eminent theophanic role of the Angel who preceded him (his *Sabiq*). Thus he was the first among all the beings to commit the twofold error which is at once that of the atheist and the orthodox believer: either he must leave the Divine in pure indetermination (*ta'til*) or else he must make It determinate. But since he failed to recognise the theophanic function of the Angel who preceded him, he inevitably had to fall into *tashbih* — and ultimately, by setting up his own predicates as those of the Unique and Supreme Divinity, he had to raise himself into a sort of Ialdaboath. The myth that in this way relates the crisis in the Pleroma to the contradiction undermining the monotheism of official exoteric religion is remarkably profound. However, this spiritual Adam-Angel is not Azaziel, even though he unknowingly harbored this Azaziel-Iblis within himself.

A medieval woodcut. On the left, St Michael spearing the dragon; in the center, the seven-headed dragon of Revelation; on the right, blood raining from heaven. The woodcut illustrates the signs of the apocalypse.

The doubt that he feels is precisely the rising to consciousness and the exteriorisation of the Darkness which had remained hidden within him, and which from then on he can conquer and hurl outside himself. In a way, he is like an archangel Michael who gains his own victory over himself, i.e. over the antagonist who had been latent within his own being. This is the 'Zervanite movement' in the Isma'ili cosmogony.[93]

I have quoted Corbin here at such length because his observations correspond in multiple ways to our discussion of the Titanic. Corbin's observations on the 'two posterities' on earth — that of the heavenly Adam, and that of Iblis-Ahriman's 'line of darkness', remind us of the constant battle between the *devas* and the *asuras*, albeit characterised in moralistic terms of good and evil. The idea of a cosmic rupture from Adam's failure to recognise the Angel who preceded him implies a kind of pre-historical Prometheanism, a 'primal lapse' out of which emerged the seven intermediate revelations within historical time. One could say that without this pre-temporal lapse, history itself would not have had an opening in which to exist. But all of these observations refer only tangentially to the Titanic.

Clearly related, though, is the central image of Corbin's discussion, that of a pre-temporal 'separation' within the primordial unity. This separating-out of the Titanic power from that which is drawn perpetually toward the Divine, is connected inevitably with that Promethean or Titanic lapse of Adam (conceived in an Angelic sense, not in some merely proto-historical sense) which meant that Adam did not 'receive' his Angelic counterpart. Here we find our focus: for this is precisely the connecting link between the esoteric 'Western' and the Eastern cosmogony.

In the doctrines of the Qabala we find reference to the emanation of creation, manifesting through the various 'degrees' or successive hierarchic *sephiroth*; and each of these *sephira* has an overflow as it were, a 'spillage' of power, and this overflow corresponds to the *sitra ahra*, or other side. This means that according to Qabalistic doctrines, the process of Creation itself — which as we will remember, is in Isma'ili doctrines a result of the primal rupture between Adam and his Angelic origin — has a direct counterpart, an 'emanation of the left hand', an hierarchy of evil, so to speak.

Gershom Scholem writes:

> According to the *Zohar*, this *sitra ahra* has ten *sephiroth* (crowns) of its own, and a similar view, albeit with several variations ... is expressed in the writings of Isaac ha-Kohen ... [who] taught that the first worlds that were destroyed were three dark emanations, which perished because of the overly concentrated power of strict judgement they contained.[94]

These three dark emanations, or previous worlds, appear to us as shells or rinds (*qlipoth*) because by the power of judgement which concluded their age (these 'worlds' in fact corresponding to previous timecycles) they are visible only in their final day of judgement — the catastrophe which concluded them. They correspond to the 'Malkhei Edom', or Kings of Edom, reference to whom we find in Genesis 3, and who are traditionally linked to an excess of *binah*, or judgement, as a result of their sins.

So to return to our theme — the metaphysical nature of the Titanic powers — we can see how the Semitic doctrines in general tend toward a moralistic interpretation which in Indian mythology is absent for the most part, a difference we remarked upon earlier. But essentially the doctrines themselves remain roughly the same: the primordial unity is divided against itself, contracts within itself (*tsim-tsum*, in Qabalistic terms), and Creation is manifested within that self-limitation of the Divine. This primordial 'dividing against itself' arises from a willing within the *Ein Soph*, the 'head of creation', not to disturb the primordial Bliss: this willing manifests as a resistance to the emanation of Creation; and this resistance was the seed of evil.

As a result — and this is true whether we speak in Isma'ili, in Qabalistic, or in Hindu terms — there is a dual posterity in humanity, a reflection of the primordial division between 'above' and 'below' for which Adam was responsible. Adam's own actions were also and necessarily a reflection of this same division which extends throughout Creation itself and makes it possible. In the cosmic drama of the 'time before time', the primordial Adam-Angel — who as we recall, in Isma'ili doctrine did not receive his preceptor Angel, and so entered into a 'lapse' which created the worlds — to put it more simply, entertained doubt, and this doubt in turn manifested as Iblis, or Ahriman, the dark power. This darkness, exteriorised and therefore recognisable, was hurled away by Adam, who himself thereby created the 'rule of Ahriman', the rule of darkness for the millennia of the world's existence. Life upon earth must necessarily be a reflection of this 'hurling away'. The dark power seeks to retard (which is also to say, to prolong the suffering which is existence, regarding existence alone as absolute), and the Angelic seeks to lead men from it, to show suffering's ultimate non-existence. The two posterities of men correspond to these two powers.

The Qabalistic tradition ameliorates the severe moralism of the exoteric tradition, which speaks purely of 'sinners' and of the 'righteous', saying rather that throughout Creation are 'sparks' of the Light, and these may be found among the evil as the good, that the *sitra ahra* also has some of the sparks. The Qabalists thereby esoterically soften the harshness of the moralism to which the Semitic faith, and its later manifestations in Christendom and Islam, tends. This moralism is absent in the Mahabharata, in which the *devas* and the *asuras* are not viewed in white and black terms, being seen rather in what we might call cyclical terms: each has his role to play in the present cycle, and though at times this role entails good on the part of the *asuras*, and deception on the part of the *devas*, their roles ultimately govern their destinies.

The Semitic moralism is valuable from a strictly human point of view, for the Fallen Angels do represent a posterity and an influence which can destroy the individual, as the race — but the work of the wise man is to join that which should be joined and separate that which should be separated.[9][5] In other words, man's task is to differentiate — in Qabalistic terms, to find the sparks where they have fallen, and raise them up. Consequently the *devas* themselves must go to the *asuras* for knowledge, just as Odin had to go to the Titan Mimir. Things in this world are invariably mixed, confused; man's task is to separate and to join in the process of restoring Paradise.

But all the same, as is made clear in *The Book of Enoch*, ultimately one must distinguish — for Divine Judgement itself distinguishes — between those of the 'dark path', and those of the Light, striving to be of the latter. In *The Book of Enoch* we read of Enoch, the scribe, being sent by the Watchers, or Fallen Angels, to ask of the Divine what their fate was to be.[9 6] God replies:

> 'Go, say to the Watchers of heaven, who have sent thee
> to intercede for them: "You should intercede for men,
> and not men for you: 3. Wherefore have ye left the high,
> holy and eternal heaven, and lain with women, and
> defiled yourselves with the daughters of men and taken
> to yourselves wives, and done like the children of earth,
> and begotten giants (as your) sons ... 6. But you were
> formerly spiritual, living the eternal life, and immortal
> for all generations of the world. 7. And therefore I have
> not appointed you wives; for as for the spiritual ones of
> the heaven, in heaven is their dwelling. 8. And now, the
> giants, who are produced from the spirits and the flesh,
> shall be called evil spirits upon the earth, and on the
> earth shall be their dwelling ... 11. And the spirits of the
> giants *afflict*, oppress, destroy, attack, do battle, and
> work destruction on the earth, and cause trouble: they
> take no food, but nevertheless hunger and thirst and
> cause offenses. 12. And these spirits shall rise up against
> the children of men and against the women, because
> they have proceeded from them ..." XVI.2. And now as to
> the Watchers who have sent thee to intercede for them
> who had been aforetime in heaven, (say to them): 3.
> "You have been in heaven, but all the mysteries had not
> yet been revealed to you, and you knew worthless ones,
> and these in the hardness of your hearts you have made
> known to the women, and through these mysteries
> women and men work much evil on earth." 4. Say
> therefore to them: "You have no peace".'[9 7]

I have quoted this passage at such length because it has
very few parallels in Judaeo-Christian apocalyptic
literature, and because it details so clearly man's
connection with the Titans. The Watchers are the Fallen
Angels, those who rebelled against heaven and sought, in
a Promethean way, to bring their limited knowledge to
mankind. Hence it is acknowledged in this tradition that
the Titans, like their progenitors the Fallen Angels, are a
source of knowledge for mankind, and perhaps even for
other beings as well. But their knowledge is necessarily
limited to the lower degrees of the mysteries, to the realm
of cosmology, the transcendent mysteries not having
been revealed to them — which suggests also the limit of
their power, for they cannot reach beyond the cosmos in

knowledge.

Here we have the connection with the giants. For what is the Titanic power but that power which, though enormous in the physical or subtle realm, cannot reach beyond the physical or the subtle? The Titans are the inheritors of the fallen angel's knowledge: they are the issue of an unnatural congress between the sons of God and the daughters of man, and hence it is said that various of the Fallen Angels are responsible for the knowledge given unto man by them: they took wives, and taught 'charms and enchantments, and the cutting of roots.'[98] Azazel taught men to 'make swords and knives and shields and breastplates, made known to them the metals of the earth, and the art of working them, bracelets and ornaments and the use of antinomy, and the beautifying of the eyelids, and all kinds of costly stones, and all colouring tinctures, as well as astrology and other kinds of knowledge, including writing.'[99]

Clearly predominant among these kinds of knowledge, though, were those of war and magic. War entails violence against man (illicit separation, division), and sorcery entails violence against heaven (illicit joining). The combination of these two led, as we have seen also in the Nordic and Indic scriptures, to a state of near-cataclysm: 'much blood was shed on earth' and 'all lawlessness' reigned.[100] The guardian Angels (Michael, Raphael, Uriel and Gabriel) looked down from heaven and saw these atrocities, and saw the souls of men, the holy ones, crying up to the gates of heaven.

They in turn petitioned the Lord of Ages to end this devastation, just as the *devas* petitioned against the reign of the *asuras*.

Thus, just as in the Mahabharata — and there is no question of influence here, for both reflect the same cosmic drama — the children of the Watchers among men are sent in battle against one another, like the two *asuras* in the myth discussed earlier, while the Fallen Angels themselves are bound in 'desert places, covered in darkness' — Semjaza and Azazel, and the others. They

Fallen Angels. A twelfth-century French-Spanish conception, in the Bibliothèque Nationale.

are to be bound for 'seventy generations', until the judgement at the end of time, after having seen their Titanic sons slay one another — and together with those Fallen Angels are to be bound all those who follow their ways, 'whosoever shall be condemned and destroyed will from thenceforth be bound together with them to the end of all generations.'[101]

Being confined to the 'valleys of the earth' as well as the banishment from the places of mankind, means that the Fallen Angels were removed to a peripheral station of being, whereby they could not directly raise havoc upon earth. This confinement corresponds to the Teutonic myths regarding the giants, of whom it is said that they live in rocks and hills or valleys, and that they are in part 'of stone', or 'of the stone age', or 'turn to stone'. One is reminded of the piles of stones and other stone monuments in Britain, Germany and elsewhere called 'giant's nests': these monuments or particular places are indeed connections with antiquity, with the stone age of the Titanic world. The swiftness of the giants (their 'seven-league boots') corresponds to the fleetness of their spiritual heritage from the Angels, and to their magical powers learnt from their progenitors the 'sons of God' (the Fallen Angels) — but their later connections with the stones implies their 'binding', and the fact that only residues of the Titanic powers still remain upon earth: those powers were exiled from earth at the close of the last timecycle.[102]

The close of the last timecycle entailed a deluge, as is made clear in the *Corpus Hermeticum*, in the Bible, and in the Norse mythology, among many sources. We have already discussed the connection between the profligate giants and the deluge implicit in the Old Testament account; but this connection is made explicit in apocryphal works like *Enoch*, which despite their non-canonicity, without question possess validity. Hence in a fragment of the Book of Noah, we read that:

> ... in the generation of Jared some of the angels
> transgressed the word of the Lord. And behold they
> commit sin and transgress the law, and have united
> themselves with women and commit sin with them, and
> have married some of them, and have begotten children
> by them. And they shall produce on the earth giants, not
> according to the spirit, but according to the flesh, and
> there shall be a great punishment on the earth, and the
> earth shall be cleansed from all impurity. Yea, there shall
> come a great destruction over the whole earth, and there
> shall be a deluge, and a great destruction for one year.
> And this son who has been born unto you shall be left on
> the earth and his three children shall be saved with
> him.[103]

This prophecy speaks, as all prophecy must, from a
timeless vision. That which has come to pass, and that
which shall come to pass, are spoken of together.
Immediately following these verses we read that after that
[deluge] man again transgressed, and transgression
followed transgression until finally an age of judgement
and then an age of righteousness came about.

That these are reflections of a greater doctrine of
timecycles is clear because earlier in *Enoch* we read that
a 'white bull' became a man, and 'built for himself a great
vessel and dwelt thereon; and three bulls dwelt with him
in that vessel.'[104] These three bulls were black, and
white, and red: and these three colours correspond to the
alchemical work; the four bulls correspond to the four
major timecycles.[105] This symbolism of the cow and the
bull has enormous primordial import, being reflected in
pre-Vedic symbolism, in Egyptian mythology, and here in
the Semitic. But here the implications are reduced to their
primal significances, being connected with the
'impregnating' or motivating stellar power or energy
which impels the entire timecycle.[106] Hence the 'stars
whose privy members were like those of horses' were
'bound hand and foot' by the Angels and 'cast into an
abyss of the earth'. The rulers of the previous era were
overcome in order that a new cycle begin, with the four
new ages (the four bulls) connected with the stars as
'motivating energies', so to speak.

This symbolism of the bull become man gives to Noah a celestial significance. The deluge clearly marks the delineation between one timecycle and the next, Noah being the captain of the ark which carries on the 'seeds' of mankind between the two. Noah is *theanthropos* (a man-god), which is to say, not a messiah, but rather man in his primordial pristine condition, man as he must appear at the end of an age, revealed in which are the 'seeds' of the next golden age. *Theanthropos* is man's natural, primordial condition.

But before this *apocatastasis* takes place — before man is restored to his primordial state — there must necessarily be a descending to the lowest point on the arc. The degradation of mankind entailed in the 'congress with giants' of the previous age must be even worse in the final age. For in the last catastrophe, that which in fact preceded our own era, man was granted a stay, so to speak, a period of time (seventy generations, says *Enoch*) at the end of which the giants shall break loose.

For as we have seen, when the Fallen Angels had dallied with human women, and had by them giants as offspring — giants who in turn destroyed the natural human harmony — the giants were murdered, so that the Fallen Angels had no direct progeny. But then, says *Enoch*, after 'the days of slaughter ... the spirits' of the giants, 'having gone forth from the souls of their flesh ... shall destroy until the day of the consummation, the great judgement in which the age shall be consummated over the Watchers and the godless, yea, shall be wholly consummated.'[107] The giants were driven from the earth in incarnate form, but were allowed to destroy still in discarnate form until the end of the age; and the Watchers, the Fallen Angels, were removed to valleys and rocky deserts, which means they were placed outside the human sphere, placed outside the cosmic wall which protects the human world from the infernal, as Midgard is protected from the forces of Ragnarok.

On this point René Guénon's discussion of the fissures in the great wall is useful. He has pointed out that the coming of judgement day necessarily entails 'fissures' through which not only the giants, but the bound Fallen Angels can find their way into the human realm again, breaking through the wall which in traditional cultures is impregnable but which, in the degree that the human world is desacralised, becomes incapable of holding back the infernal. According to Guénon:

> In Islamic tradition these 'fissures' are those by which, at cycle's end, the devastating hordes of Gog and Magog will force their way in, for they are unremitting in their efforts to invade this world; these 'entities' represent the inferior influences in question. They are considered as maintaining an underground existence, and are described both as giants and as dwarfs; they may thus be identified, in accordance with what was said earlier on the subject, and at least in certain connections, with the 'guardians of the hidden treasure', and with the smiths of the 'subterranean fire' who have, it may be recalled, an exceedingly maleficent aspect; in all such symbolisms the same kind of 'infracorporeal' subtle influences are really always involved.[108]

Guénon emphasizes the malevolent aspect of the giants and dwarves, and this is indisputably accurate with regard to our present humanity — we have already seen how, from a wider and more distant perspective like that glimpsed in the Mahabharata, and even in the Norse myths, the giants or *danavas* (this being in remote antiquity, when congress among different stations of being was much more fluid) also had pious beings among their number. However, their Promethean, or Luciferian spirit finally drove them to commit all manner of outrages upon the earth, leading finally to their banishment; and so they must remain among the infernal, destructive powers, among the legions whose provenance is destruction.

This connection is after all only natural — for if the giants were there at Creation, preceding even man in this timecycle, it is by laws of complementary balance necessary that they be at the end as well, for end and beginning are invariably connected. After all, Titanic powers come into play primarily in creation and destruction; for harmony to flourish, they must be kept at bay, under control. Hence in fact the giants are connected — in traditions so completely disparate as to have had no possible contact save in a primordial culture of such antiquity as to be wholly outside the scope of our consideration — always to the numbers nine, and eighteen thousand (the zeros being, in traditional number-symbolism, of virtually no meaning whatever). Why should they be connected to these numbers specifically?

Chiefly, the answer is this: the Titans or *asuras* are, as we have seen, consanguine with Creation itself; the Titanic powers are connected with the cosmos in folklore and mythology over all the world, and their insurrection cannot rise above the Hermetic 'three worlds'. This is why in all the various mythologies, the Titans are said to at times possess the 'nectar of immortality', but at no time can they become immortal. As is written in *Enoch*, they desire eternal life, but they may not have it. Hence they are limited to this cosmos — this is why they desire, too, to enter into the human world once again: they wish to live in that centrality peculiar to the earthly human state. But even if they do enter that world, they cannot attain to the spiritual, for they are by their very nature incapable.

The 'three worlds' are the Titans' purview; and nine and eighteen correspond to this as multiples of three, being therefore an indication of all contingencies within these three primal spheres; and eighteen thousand is an indication of indefinite potentiality. In Norse mythology there are 'nine worlds' on the Tree Yggdrasil; and this comprises the whole of manifestation. But the tree's roots are the three worlds of giants, humans and misty Hel, so we can see that the nine are an extrapolation of the three. In the Qabala we find that there are eighteen thousand worlds, forty-five hundred in each of the four directions (which we must note is divisible by nine and three also), and 'these eighteen thousand worlds are then surrounded by fire and water' ... beyond which circles are finally 'nothing but night without end, without number, without quality or quantity.'[109]

Likewise in the *Shan Hai Ching*, or 'Hill and River Classic', we read that the giants live in their own country barred from the human by iron gates, and that, covered with black hair, they live for eighteen thousand years. Fierce creatures, they are known to eat human flesh, primarily after battles; and there are certain openings to the human world along the mountains of North-eastern Asia through which they may pass, at which the human and Titanic worlds may intersect.[110] Similar European legends about the Titans or giants refer to their having nine heads, or three heads, and these correspond to Tityos, son of earth, said in Homer's *Odyssey* to cover nine roods, while Ephialtes and Otos were nine fathoms tall, in their ninth year;[111] and Dante, in the *Inferno*, describes Nimrod at 90 palms (54 feet).[112] Likewise, Polish legends refer explicitly to the *dziewie-sil* (nine-powered) giants of old, 'power', after all, being more accurate than 'head', which is simply a way of expressing powers or potentialities.

As we saw earlier, there are in the Norse myths seen to be nine degrees or stations of being on the Tree of Life; and the Titans' identification with nine or with the eighteen-thousand worlds corresponds to their consanguinity with all the possibilities of creation. Though the Titans have been banished from the earth, they are nonetheless — by way of traces or residues inherent in the stones and the valleys — in the caves; which is to say, their traces permeate all creation down to the depths of matter itself. They are indivisible from the whole of Creation, for they are (as we recall the giant Ymir's, or Yama's, role in Creation) the Titanic powers from which the various worlds were made, or rather, the 'rinds' (*qlipoth*) of those powers.

That this is the significance of the number nine's connection to the Titans is clarified by a Chinese myth which speaks of Niu-kua, sister and wife of Fo-hi, who melted stones of five colours in order to repair a rent in the terrestrial horizon made by a Titan. When it is recalled that Fo-hi, who reigned jointly with her, set the earth upon the four legs of the tortoise, we recognise the symbolism of nine: the four directions combine with the five elements; spatiality is combined with the qualitative or elemental aspects of creation within that spatiality.[1 1 3] The Titans are the 'residue' of the powers of Creation, and hence are identified with nine as a kind of 'reversal': the power they represent was that of creation, but those same powers reversed are those of destruction, and towards this the Titans inevitably move.

This accounts for the identification, early in the Mahabharata, of the *asuras* with the *devas*; and for their later 'reversal', which made of them the *devas'* implacable enemies. We must remember that as a timecycle continues, all the accumulated error and sin and confusion which man has generated feeds the *sitra ahra* or 'other side', the *qlipoth* or 'residue' of creation. Early in a timecycle evil is not quite so powerful — hence one has the golden age. But as the cycle continues on, all the evil that man does reinforces the destructive powers, which in turn reinforce the evil which man does. This is why, at the 'end of time', it is prophesied in many traditions that 'brother shall act against siblings and parents', that death and destruction shall be over the land.

For man is not separate from the rest of Creation, and indeed to a very great degree Creation depends upon man. Hence the indisseverability of man and timecycle; for the way man relates to the cosmos is indivisible from the manifestations of that timecycle. Without man one could not have an 'end of time' (which is to say, end of a timecycle), for because of man's centrality in the cosmos, all the manifestations of a given timecycle correspond to his relation to the cosmos. Hence in the golden age man is in total harmony with heaven and with the earth; in the iron age, man is in utter disharmony with everything.

This means that the Titanic forces, those hordes that

wish to rush in through the 'fissures in the great wall', must necessarily enter into the human world. For only through the destruction of the traditional religious traditions and the sacred sphere which surrounds them (which protects our world from the infernal), can the Titanic powers wreak the havoc that signals the end of this world, and the creation of a new.

Creation and destruction are in a very profound sense indivisible: the destruction of one world is its purification, as well as the creation of a new, freed from the dross accumulated in a world run down, a world become senile and destructive, cold and lifeless, quantified and barren. The work of the Titans is, from a limited perspective, malevolent: it entails the destruction of our present society and the present mankind (for they are the warriors in the battle at the end of time, the battle for Jambhala, the Northern Gates to Heaven, after all). But from a much wider perspective, one detached from partiality toward our current society, such a destruction is neither more nor less than a purification of our world, 'world' here being ultimately limited to the human realm, though because of human centrality, extending necessarily throughout life on our planet and the subtle realms as well.

In great antiquity — far beyond the bounds of profane history — the Titans were beneficent. But in nearer antiquity, like that recorded in the Celtic and Norse myths, the Titans were divided into two camps, the good giants and the Frost giants, corresponding in some respects to the Celtic Túatha Dé Danaan and the Fomorians. In all the accounts referring to the battle at the end of time, the bound *asuras* or Antigods lead their Titanic forces against the Divine citadel: Loki leads the hordes of giants against Asgard, just as in the second battle of Mag Tuired, Bres forsakes the Gods and joins the Fomorians; and just, for that matter, as Lucifer forsakes the Angelic for the Ahrimanic or Satanic rule in the cosmic drama.

But this battle at the end of time does not end the

cosmos: a new mankind, and a new earth are born, causally connected with the old, but purified, freed of the error, sin, confusion and ignorance that characterised the old. Hence in the Vafpruonismál we read that in the renewed world, the 'wise maidens who travel over the sea' are 'the only guardian spirits upon earth, kindred of giants', and they arrive in three companies, again recalling the connections between the giants and the three worlds. Likewise, in the Voluspa, we read that at the beginning of the world, three maidens come from the sea to guard the earth. This connection of end and beginning, of destruction and creation, is reinforced in the Norse myths, in which Njord, a Titan taken hostage by the Aesir (the Gods) in an earlier battle, returns to the Vanir or Titans at the end of time, and in the new or purified world the Vanir are again restored to their original high place, and the old Gods are gone. This restitution must take place: for there can be no golden age if a restitution of the fallen ones does not occur. Origen was not wrong to argue that Lucifer must be redeemed also at the end of the ages: the cosmic drama must return full circle to its inception.

There are those who already prepare the way for this *apocatastasis*, some of whom are conscious of their function, others of whom are not. Among those perfectly aware of what they do are those affiliated with certain heretical teachers, who have explicitly identified themselves with the *dralas*, or 'enemies of the Gods'; and with the lineage of the Fallen Angels, which indeed amount to different terms for the same thing. Others 'prepare the way' for the end without being aware of their function, and among these no doubt are those who prepare the Titanic forces of war to be unleashed upon the earth, weapons of fire and of infinite suffering.

Yet to truly understand our situation, we must recur to a Tibetan teaching, that of the kingdom of Jambhala, ruled by Kubera and existing in the North. Jambhala is the opening, upon this earth, of the central 'channel' to the celestial forces emanating from the cosmic Center or

Tree or Axis. For this reason North, or more properly, North-east, is essential in Taoist magic, as also in certain Amerindian and Shamanic traditions.[114] Those who live in Jambhala — to which there are 'openings' in certain Asian mountain valleys — live essentially in the golden age, in absolute harmony and delight, for many years, perfecting themselves on the way to enlightenment. According to Tibetan teachings, though, at the end of time the *asuras* will seek to overcome the citadel, seek to dominate the kingdom; and mankind, the Gods and all manner of beings will be embroiled in a vast battle at the end of time, a battle which corresponds with Isaiah's mention of Lucifer and the North in the Bible — once again a cryptic Judaeo-Christian reference to a much vaster teaching.

The battle for Jambhala will be prefaced, however, by infinitely increased suffering upon earth, and a corresponding intensification of technology — mankind will perfect materialistic power, in concert with a despoliation of the earth and of fellow men. Suffering is simply the gap between the way things are, and the way one feels things ought to be. So one can easily see how, in a world which bases itself upon mere power over material phenomena, the potential for suffering is vastly increased. Man who cares nothing for possessing the things of this world is not likely to suffer over mere gain or loss.

This increased suffering is perceived by Tara — 'she who hears the cries of the world' (Jap.: Kanzeon) — and finally she hypostatises as a lama, who tells the leaders of the Titanic human world about Jambhala, thereby hastening their attack upon it. The Titans wish to overcome Jambhala, the last Divine stronghold in the human world. The subsequent battle is, in Christian terms, equivalent to The Apocalypse. Only through this beneficent purification can the suffering of these end times be concluded, and the subsequent golden age manifest.

The attempts of the Titanically inspired human world to overcome Jambhala, to enter the Divine citadel, correspond to the Hindu myth of Rahu and Ketu, the *danavas* (giants) who sought to eat the *amrita* (the nectar of immortality), and who were decapitated, their heads then trying to consume the sun and the moon in eclipses. This eclipse of the Divine corresponds to the final days of a world, when the Divine sun is eclipsed. Not for nothing did the Celts, the Norsemen, the Egyptians and the Amerindians all fear the day when the sun should go away, when disharmony reigns in every sphere.

But at the same time we must recall that the eclipse is necessarily only temporary and cyclical, that the disharmony it creates will certainly pass, and that the Divine sun is by no means blotted out forever, nor can it be. What is more, as the Tibetan Buddhist myth of Tara hastening the final battle out of concern for the suffering of all beings demonstrates, we should not fear but rather welcome this end to the vast, vast suffering that now characterises our world.

There is no need to fear the Fallen Angels, the *asuras*, the Titans: they, like all beings, have a special place in the hierarchy of being, and a specific function to perform in the cycles of the worlds. It is far better to understand that place than to live in ignorance of those forces which at this very moment control our world. For we are caught among the currents of forces man in the modern world is wholly incapable of comprehending: though we may conceive of our world as wholly physical, it is in truth a tiny outpost amidst cataclysmic forces and beings beyond our conception, for whom we are nonetheless center stage. Man must follow the middle way because he is in the center of the cosmos, because as microcosm all the vast forces of creation and destruction have their sway within him also, and because upon him, upon his religious vocation, and the realisation of spiritual liberation on this precarious earthly island depends all the cosmos.

The forces of creation and destruction in this cosmos are indivisibly linked. The Titans are instinct with creation, indeed 'preceding' man himself; and they are instinct with destruction; they are, ultimately, indivisible from the multifaceted nature of this cosmos itself. From a limited purview we could call them, and their progenitors — the Fallen Angels without whom the cosmos itself could not exist (for they are the 'cause' in one sense, and the 'effect' in another of the 'Divine lapse', the contraction which is the drama of Creation) — 'evil'. But the Fallen Angels are necessary for the celestial drama which is existence in all its potentialities to play itself out: without them, neither we nor this celestial drama could exist, so integral are they to it.

Our place in this celestial drama is in one sense determined, and in another our choice: but in either case our ultimate aim must be, not choosing the good or the bad, but rather attaining that liberation which is the *summa* of not merely all human endeavors but of all existence. For only thus can our true purpose, our true nature, and the meaning of all the celestial drama come truly clear to us: without realising liberation, the 'crown of existence', we are but the pawns of vast forces. With liberation, we too engage in the play of the cosmos, but are not attached.

Chapter VI
Devas and Angels:
Dance of the Stars

In his *Spiritual Canticle*, St. John of the Cross speaks of how, to men and Angels alike, God is like 'strange islands'. He says:

> It is no wonder that God is strange to men who have not seen Him, since He is also strange to the holy angels and to the blessed. For the angels and the blessed are incapable of seeing Him fully, nor will they ever be capable of doing so. Until the day of the Last Judgement they will see so many new things in Him concerning His deep judgements and His works of mercy and justice that they will forever be receiving new surprises and marveling the more. Hence not only men but also the angels can call Him strange islands. Only to Himself is He neither strange nor new.[115]

In this commentary the Angels and the blessed of men are placed on an equal level; but St. John of the Cross is here speaking of them by comparison to the infinite mystery of the Divine. In such a comparison, the Angels and men are both as nil. But nonetheless, if we reverse the perspective, and view the Angelic from the human perspective rather than from the Divine by projection, we can speak to some considerable extent about the nature of the Angels and of the nature of the *devas* or gods, in Eastern traditions.

Of the Angels, Roger Bacon in his *Opus Majus* VII.1 says the following: 'besides corporeal things, God has formed spiritual substances which we call Intelligences and Angels; for Intelligence is the name of a nature, and

Angel is the name of a function.' But to understand this very condensed statement, we have to consider its underpinnings in the works of St. Dionysius the Areopagite, and the Platonic hierarchies more generally.

The Intelligences are, in Platonic terms, those natures which participate directly in the Divine mind, directly in the apprehension of the celestial Essences (quiddities) of things. We spoke earlier of the celestial Axis: in this Axis, in the hierarchy of being, the Intelligences are 'above' the human station, freed of corporeality and the suffering it entails, and, like the stars, the Intelligences bathe in and irradiate the primordial light of the Divine. And the Angelic is in essence a term denoting the function of the Intelligences, which is to say, their *irradiative* nature in relation to the human world, and all 'below' them in the celestial hierarchy. They at once participate in the Divine, and in turn they irradiate that in which they participate.

Thus, says St. Dionysius the Areopagite, the celestial beings have 'abundant communion' with God, receiving 'the Primal Radiance in a pure and immaterial manner, adapting themselves to this in a life wholly intellectual.' 'Wherefore they are above all pre-eminently worthy of the name Angel because they first receive the Divine Light, and through them are transmitted to us the revelations which are above us.'[116] 'It is thus that the Law (as written in the Scriptures) was given us by Angels, and both before and after the days of the Law, Angels guided our illustrious forefathers to God,' and this, he continues, is only natural, for 'the higher are initiators and guides of the lower to the divine approach, illumination and union.'[117]

As Plotinus wrote, 'It is necessary that everything impart itself to something else; or the Good will not be good, nor Intellect be intellect, nor Soul be soul; unless after that which lives primarily there is also that which has a secondary life.'[118] Of course, the human is not necessarily secondary to the Angelic, for the human being is also possessed of a spiritual essence. But the human being is sunken in the mire of temporality, of suffering, and hence this essence is obscured, so that although the human potential is for 'celestial nobility' and the human may be a 'mirror reflecting the Divine', by virtue of temporal existence this mirror is occluded. And hence the Angelic function, from the human perspective, is to guide and to initiate.

The question, of course, is the degree to which the spiritual substance of man corresponds to and relates to the Angelic. Ibn Arabi has written in this regard:

> Man surpasses the other species of the elementary domain only because he is 'kneaded' by the Divine 'Two Hands'; it is from that that his species is more noble than any other species formed by the elements without this double Divine touch (which corresponds to the 'central' nature of man); that is to say that man possesses a dignity superior to that of the terrestrial angels (amongst whom are the genii) as also the celestial Angels (populating the seven celestial spheres, formed of subtle modalities of the elements) whereas the superior Angels are better than the human species, according to the sacred text (since they did not have to prostrate themselves before Adam).[119]

Ibn Arabi does not here differ in any significant way from St. Dionysius the Areopagite, but in this quotation we are given to understand the relative stations of the Angels and of man more clearly. That is, in the Angelic, stations of being can be of various modalities: those Angels who are superior to men are those referred to by St. Dionysius in the *Celestial Hierarchies*; but there are other modalities, including some, like the *jinn*, which we have mentioned, and which are parallel to the human station, though they do not participate in corporeality nor in the human centrality therefore.

Then, too, there are the Angels of the 'seven celestial spheres'; these correspond to the creation of the seven planets. Now these seven celestial spheres correspond to subtle reality, or to the mediate world 'between' the Transcendent and the temporal realms, and this is why we can speak of the planetary spheres in terms of personality, speaking of Mars as angry or fiery, of Jupiter as benign or beneficent, of Mercury as changeable, and so forth. These traditional assignations to the planets are by no means arbitrary, but rather correspond to very real aspects of subtle reality which figure in the human personality because of the human nature as microcosm, reflecting in its centrality all the myriad aspects of the cosmos as a whole. These seven celestial spheres also irradiate their influences — just as do all the Angels, this being as we have seen their functional nature — but rather than being purely spiritual, these influences make up the warp and weft of all things on earth, everything having its 'divine signature' which reflects the various planetary modalities. Hence the seven spheres are extremely important to traditional medicine — but to detail this would take a treatise in itself.[1 2 0]

The various modalities of being we term Angelic here vary considerably, but they do all share in common their incorporeality, from whence comes at once their freedom from the suffering which characterises the human condition; and their correspondent (in the seven spheres and terrestrial conditions) non-centrality by comparison to the human. Additionally, however, those stations of being comprising the seven spheres and the celestial orders, from the human perspective correspond to initiatory stations, and thus René Guénon could write in his *The Multiple States of the Being*:

> It follows from what we have said that we can understand by "spiritual hierarchies" nothing other than the ensemble of the states of being which are superior to the human individuality, and more especially to the non-formal or supra-individual states. We can still regard these states as realisable by the being from a human basis, and this even in the course of its corporeal and terrestrial existence. This realisation is in effect implied in the totalisation of the being, that is, in "Deliverance" (*Moksha* or *Mukti*) by which the being is freed from the ties of every special condition of existence ... But if the goal to be reached is the same for all beings, each will of course achieve it according to his "personal way," hence by modalities susceptible to indefinite variations.[1 2 1]

Naturally the 'terrestrial angels' are not among those initiatory stations, being as they are horizontal to the human condition; but the seven celestial spheres colour the human perception of the initiatory ascent, since one must 'pass through' them.

On the nature of the planets, or 'mobile stars', Titus Burckhardt writes:

> The heaven of the fixed stars, which is contained in the sphere of the 'towers' of the Zodiac, is called the heaven of the 'stations' (*manazil*), because the movements of the planets project themselves upon it. The seven planets which represent the cosmic intermediaries between the immutable world of the archetypes and the earthly centre, actualise, by their combined rhythms and the reciprocal positions which ensue, the spatial relations virtually contained in the indefinite sphere of the sky-limit, the sphere being no other than the totality of the directions of the space, and hence the image of the universe.[1 2 2]

In other words, the planets are mediate between the earth and the heaven of the fixed stars and, by implication, mediate between man and the Angelic: as we said before, the planets colour or tinge that which shines through them from 'above'; this is the meaning of their place in the 'initiatory ascent' to which Guénon refers.

The Angelic corresponds, strictly speaking, to the ocean 'above the heavens', and the stars are the figuring forth of this ocean of supercelestial bliss, the perpetual *contemplatio divinis*. Hence, says Pico della Mirandola in his *Heptaplus*:

> Since ... the highest hierarchy has leisure only for contemplation, it is properly symbolised by the waters that are placed above the heavens, that is, above all action in regard to worldly things, whether heavenly or earthly, and they praise God unceasingly with everlasting sound. Since the middle rank is assigned to the work of the heavens, it could not be more fittingly symbolised than by the firmament, that is, the sky. The final hierarchy, although by nature it is above everybody and above the heavens, nevertheless has charge of all things under the heavens. Since it is divided into

principalities, archangels and angels, all the activity of these is concerned only with what is under the moon. [1] [2] [3]

Mirandola is here basing himself upon the Dionysian hierarchies, of which we spoke earlier, but he makes explicit that which in Dionysius himself is only implicit — the connection between the Angelic and the 'waters above'.

The 'waters above' must be understood, again, not in any physicalised sense but as the supra-formal ocean of bliss which is 'around' the emanatory Divine Center of the cosmos. All the Angels participate in this ocean by their nature, some more so than others, according to the hierarchies to which we have alluded earlier.

Thus far we have considered only the Angelic, which is to say, only the supra-human aspects of the cosmic axis, from the Western perspective, and at this point we should like to turn to the Eastern understanding of the same hierarchic cosmology. To begin, we must emphasize a chief difference between the two: whereas from the more exoteric Judaeo-Christian view generally (not quite so much from the Islamic, particularly not the Sufic understanding, which participates much more in an Oriental initiatory perspective) the celestial hierarchies are perceived from a 'passive' view. Admittedly man is guided by the Angelic, as St. Dionysius had it, but the Angelic irradiates the celestial nature. By contrast — and we say this primarily as reference to a different view of the same truth — in Buddhism particularly, the celestial stations are perceived not necessarily in the relatively anthropomorphised forms of Angels, but as stations of meditative absorption, or *dhyanas*.

Of course we say 'not necessarily' because, despite what we just said, there are many parallels indeed between the Buddhist and the Judaeo-Christian celestial hierarchies. Not only do the Upper Waters referred to in Judaeo-Christian and Hindu traditions correspond in many respects to the Realm of Non-form (*arupyadhatu*) at the top of the Buddhist vertical cosmology, but what is more, the *devas* in Buddhist tradition correspond to the Angels in Judaeo-Christian tradition.

We have already seen how in the Christian tradition the Angelic is conceived in terms of hierarchies: one has the Angels, Archangels and Principalities, the Dominions, Virtues and Powers, and finally the Cherubim, Seraphim and Thrones, these three groupings corresponding to purification (the lower hierarchies); illumination (the middle or heavenly hierarchies); and perfection (the supermundane hierarchies).[124] The same is true in Buddhist tradition: in the *cakravala*, or 'one-world' vertical cosmology, one has three realms also: the *kamadhatu* (realm of desire); the *rupadhatu* (realm of form); and the *arupyadhatu* (formless realm).

What is more, just as the Angels of the lower heaven have dominion over worldly things (principalities), so too in Buddhist cosmology the *kamadeva*, or Gods of Desire, include the Four Great Kings, the Blissful Gods, and Yama, among others. The Four Great Kings, not surprisingly, are the most numerous of all the Gods, inhabiting as they do the palaces (*vimana*) of the sun, moon and stars.[125] In this, once again, they correspond quite well to the Christian principalities. Their function is similar as well: envisaged as meditative stations, the *kamadeva* represent the purifying of human desires (which is the implication of Yama, whose function as ruler of the dead is obviously that of purification).

Likewise, just as the function of the Dominions, Virtues and Powers is illumination, so too the *devas* of the realm of form, or 'middle realm', are called *abhasvara* or 'radiant Gods', *apramanabha* or 'immeasurable splendour', and so forth. Conceived in terms of beauty and light, the beings of the *rupadhatu* (realm of form) are freed from gross desire and exist illuminant, as do the Angels of the middle realm. But at the 'top' of the realm of form, in the fourth *dhyana* or absorption, we find that the stations there are conceived not as positive, or illuminant, being rather negative — i.e. no effort, no heat, no clouds and so forth. This is by way of transition to the highest realm, that of formlessness, which is characterised in four stages:

IV. Neither Consciousness nor Non-consciousness
III. Realm of No-thing
II. Intellectual Infinitude
I. Spatial Infinitude[1 2 6]

These characterisations by way of negation correspond to the Christian realm of the Seraphim, Cherubim and Thrones, who are 'filled with Light higher than all immaterial knowledge and rapt, as is meet, in the contemplation of that Beauty which is the super-essential triune Origin and Creator of all Beauty.'[1 2 7] Hence 'in perpetual purity they encompass His eternal Knowledge in that most high and eternal angelic dance, rapt in the bliss of manifold blessed contemplations, and irradiated with pure and primal splendours.'[1 2 8]

This language is more analogical than the Buddhist terms — one does not find the *arupyadhatu* described as a dance — but there are again, here, manifest correspondences between the Christian and the Buddhist understandings. For instance, the terms of St. Dionysius — contemplations, rapt, filled with Light higher than immaterial knowledge — correspond to human perceptions, and indicate implicitly what is explicit in the Buddhist understanding: all of these stations may be realised by the human being by way of *dhyana*, or meditative absorption.

So although the Christian view of the Angelic tends toward the representational rather than toward the experiential, though it tends to emphasize the human being as receiver rather than as he who realises these stations, still these divergences with the Buddhist emphasis upon meditative experientiality are more apparent than real. The correspondences between the two traditions regarding the devic or Angelic realms are quite extraordinary in fact, as we have seen.

Correspondences like this led nineteenth-century European writers on comparative religion to postulate actual influence of one religion upon the other; but we hardly need do that, for clearly both reflect the same primordial truth. Naturally, there are divergences in approach. In some respects, Christianity seems to have forgotten its primordial vision as manifested in St. Dionysius the Areopagite's *Celestial Hierarchies*, and to have lost — speaking here of its Western variants, rather than of the Eastern Orthodox — the initiatory path it must proffer if it is to be a complete tradition, and not simply an exoteric faith exhorting the masses to virtuous conduct. Hence Christianity appears to be a more 'passive' tradition than Buddhism, for example, in that the Angels seem like Divine functionaries only, rather than stations of Divine emanation which man, in his initiatory 'ascent of the Axis', can realise.

In any case we have only touched on three major traditions — Buddhism and Christianity, and between them Islam — in this discussion of the Angelic. But by way of this discussion we hope the reader has at least grasped the essential meaning of devic or Angelic reality. The *devas* are, for our purposes of analysis here, the same as Angels; and both represent stations of ascent upon the Divine Axis, the initiatory path which man must follow to liberation. Of course there are Angelic beings who are horizontal to man, and hence do not represent initiatory stations (the *jinn*, for instance — terrestrial angels). There are beings superior to man who do not represent stations on the Axis for him, but who in their sidereal splendour and delight, reflect and irradiate the Divine. However, we have here dwelt upon those stations directly relating to the human condition, for it is with that we must necessarily be principally concerned. Our focus in this work on traditional cosmology is, in other words, not simply a disinterested survey of cosmologies, but is intended to point man toward the one thing needful, toward spiritual liberation, realisation.

But before we turn to this latter topic, let us consider — heaven.

Chapter VII
Paradise and Heaven

To speak of paradise or heaven in any single way is difficult, for so much depends upon the perspective and the tradition in question. In Hinduism, for instance, particularly from the Vedantic perspective, paradise as *svargaloka* or 'region of light' is by no means the 'end' and purpose of human existence, but rather is a station high among the transmigrationist possibilities for a being, the result of one's virtuous *karma*. Conversely, in Judaeo-Christian traditions generally, heaven is the aim of human life. One does find mystics like Meister Eckhart, or Jan van Ruysbroeck, insisting upon the primacy of complete transcendence, upon dissolving in the 'simple nakedness' of the 'dazzling darkness' of the Divine, but the majority of Christians have never heard of this, and seek not spiritual realization in this life, but heaven or paradise after death. Then again, one has the Buddhist Pure Land tradition, in which the aim of the practitioner is to realize a place in *Sukhavati*, the Pure Land, after death or even in this very life. All of these traditions seem so very different that one can hardly see the parallels, and the idea of 'paradisal reward' seems very ambiguous indeed. But, as we shall see, it is possible to attain a general understanding of paradise and of heaven, and of their places in traditional cosmology.

To begin, one must differentiate between these two terms 'paradise' and 'heaven'. By its nature, the conception of paradise entails an individual or a being to realise it: paradise is invariably considered, by the various

Tree of the Angels. From a Persian miniature, Fabriz school, mid-16th century, showing a garden of paradise.

traditions, as a reward for the being's virtuous, unwavering conduct in the face of temptation and suffering. But being virtuous is also a precondition for the being that reaches beyond the rewards of paradisal bliss, to realise the heavenly stations of transcendence from which there is no return. For traditionally — drawing on both Hindu and Christian traditions — we may speak of two celestial posthumous human conditions, separated by the 'gateway of the Sun': first, there is the paradise attained by believers, by the virtuous; and second, there is the heaven of the 'knower', he who has realised the Truth 'beyond the Sun-door'.

This is what is meant in the New Testament, when in Luke 23:43, Christ said to one of the 'malefactors' who were being crucified with him: 'Verily I say unto thee: today thou shalt be with me in paradise.' The thief upon the cross is in the paradise that lasts until the close of the age, and the day of judgement — he is not in heaven; he has not attained an angelic state. As Christ said in John 14:2-3, 'In my Father's house are many mansions: if it were not so, I would have told you. I go to prepare a place for you. And if I go and prepare a place for you, I will come again, and receive you unto myself; that where I am, there ye may be also.' In this earthly life we prepare our own afterlife, be it in a paradise, or in heaven, or elsewhere. Christ will receive us to the degree we have realized His transcendent state in ourselves — for the Kingdom is not without, but within. The thief has his place in a paradise; the saint has his place in heaven. Hence in the Bhagavad Gita we read:

> *Brahma-nirvana* is attained by those seers whose sins are no more. Doubts gone, minds steady, they rejoice in the welfare of every being. [1] [2] [9]

This refers to those who are liberated from suffering. On the other hand, of those who attain paradise, we read:

> Having enjoyed paradise's vast realm, they return to the human world, merit exhausted;
> Those who follow the three Vedas, desirous of

enjoyments, win only the changeable.[130]

Clearly one sees here two stations: first, we see the possibility of transcendence in Brahman, and second we see the cyclical rise to paradise and fall from it. Now to attain *Brahma-nirvana* is to attain the very station of Brahma, to become Brahman, but those beings who enter the *svarga-loka*, or 'paradisal realm of light', because they are still in the realm of transmigration, eventually will pass again from this existence into yet another in the rounds of being. 'Paradise' here in Hindu tradition is a blissful incorporeal state from which one will again fall.

By contrast, although in the Judaeo-Christian and Islamic traditions paradise is represented often in spatio-temporal terms, it is an intermediate posthumous state that lasts until the 'close of the age', and translation into heaven, when the things of this earth pass away. In spatial terms paradise is conceived as light, as vastness, as great wealth and beauty, even in more specific terms of beautiful women, beautiful landscape, musical waters, and the like. In temporal terms, it is generally conceived as eternity, the extension of the being's delight-filled experientiality into infinitude. The Islamic paradises correspond to both of these, as does the Christian, and the Jodo Shinshu Buddhist Pure Land embraces also certain spatial symbolism including the 'celestial lake', the lotuses afloat in it, representing the faithful, the celestial landscape of *Sukhavati*, and so forth. In all of these one sees the 'extension' or the 'fruition' of the individual in a paradisal state that lasts until the closing of the age, or Divine re-absorption, and translation into the Inconceivable.

The difference we have so far elaborated corresponds also to Egyptian doctrines in this respect. 'Paradise' as a contingent cosmological station corresponds to the realms of Osiris as elaborated in the *PER EM HRU*, or the 'Book of the Coming Forth by Day', the Theban rescension of the Book of the Dead. But the followers of Amen-Ra entered into the 'Boat of Millions of Years', were transmuted into the 'light of Ra', and never returned to a temporal sphere. The followers of Osiris entered into the Osirian paradise to find a celestial earth, their celestial existence corresponding to the life of the Buddhist Gods who, by way of thought, by way of magic, obtain anything good they desire.

This Osirian existence is in its nature contingent upon remaining in that station of the cosmos, whereas the 'Boat of Millions of Years', the paradise of Amen-Ra, is 'hidden' and 'beyond' the transmutation from one cosmic station to another. Those who enter the Osirian paradise do so by passing through the 'balance of judgement', which is to say by way of good *karma*; whereas those who realise the state of light in the heaven of Amen-Ra have, through celestial knowledge, passed beyond the realms in which 'judgement' obtains.[131]

So man's posthumous condition may answer to several possibilities: he may realise the heavenly stations; he may realise the 'realm of paradisal light' (from a lower state of which he may fall; while from a higher state he may realize the Inconceivable); he may enter limbo, or the bardo, an intermediate station 'during' transmigration; or he may enter purgatory or hell. These all are cosmological stations, hence part of the 'round of birth and death', save heaven, or *Brahma-nirvana* which is, as its name implies, the transmutation of the being into a wholly different order — although one cannot call this absolute liberation, it being still conditional under the name *Brahma*. All of the other stations are subject to indefinite modulation, and the being may pass from one to another according to his *karma*, his merit or demerit.

Thus paradise, in its 'terrestrial' or 'lowest' form, corresponds to the fruition of a being's meritorious *karma*, and is an exhaustible condition, while in the 'higher paradises' one continues on toward heaven, or absolute transcendence. Traditionally in Vedic terms, then, the term 'lower paradise' may be used to denote the 'paradise of Indra', which is the highest of the three worlds (*svah*), but still therefore part of the cycle of birth and death. This is, says Coomaraswamy, 'a [paradise] accessible to all who have done good works, irrespective of understanding, and whence there is for them a constant coming back to terrestrial conditions.'[1 3 2]

This is not so of the higher paradises, or the Empyrean heaven: for when a being passes beyond the 'gateway of the Sun', there is no return (*punar avrtti*), and though this is not, again, absolute liberation, it is transcendence 'beyond time', corresponding to the Angelic supermundane existence. Thus in the Chandogya Upaniṣad we find that as quickly as the knower directs his thought after death, does he come to the 'world door' of the Sun, beyond which is 'unlimited freedom'.[1 3 3] St. Thomas Aquinas writes that 'man can merit glory in such a degree as to be equal to the angels, in each of the angelic grades; and this implies that men are taken up into the orders of the angels.'[1 3 4] Likewise, says Eckhart, 'the man who is exalted above time into eternity will do with God what he did in the past and also what he does in the next thousand years ... meaning that in eternity, exalted above time, man does one work with God.'[1 3 5]

There is an apparent divergence here between the Christian and the Hindu doctrines under discussion, in that the latter presume transmigrationist possibilities for the being, whereas Christianity tends to represent the posthumous states in a more absolute way. But these may be to a considerable extent resolved if we recognise that Christianity offers a condensed or 'crystallised' religious understanding, and by emphasizing the essentiality of this life turns man toward his religious purpose, toward 'the one thing needful' with more intensity than if the wider and more diffusing, though not incompatible truths of transmigration were included within it. The existence of the different Angelic stations, and hence of different 'kinds' or 'degrees' of heaven and of paradise within Christianity certainly imply other possibilities than simply translation into a single eternal station after a single life.

Thus far, then, we have simply distinguished between

heaven, or the 'immortality' of the Angels, and paradise;
the former affiliated with Brahman, the latter with Indra
(with therefore the illusion of individuality). This is the
fundamental difference between the celestial posthumous
possibilities for mankind, regardless in fact of the
tradition in question. So let us then turn from Hindu and
Christian teachings to Buddhist teachings regarding
heaven and Paradise, for this will allow us to extend
those distinctions we have already made.

The Buddhist *Sukhavati*, or Pure Land, is a heavenly
station of being intermediate, so to speak, between the
complete transcendence of the Buddhas, who are wholly
realised beings, and the relative 'darkness' or confusion of
beings in the samsaric vortex. Created by the salvific
power of Amitabha Buddha, it is a station of being freed
of suffering, in which beings are transmuted — there is,
from it, no return to the samsaric vortex as there is from
certain of the paradisal stations, but at the same time the
beings in it are not so wholly transmuted as to be beyond
conception as beings at all, as are the Buddhas.

In the Sukhavativyuha the Pure Land of *Sukhavati* is
described to Ananda, a disciple of the Buddha, and there
are a number of points which we should here note in that
description. First, we can see that this is a heavenly
realm: there are countless jewels and jewel-trees,
countless vast lotus-flowers, from each of which issue
countless Buddhas in rays, manifesting thus the
Buddhadharma in countless world-systems. Every aspect
of this bliss-world manifests the Divine, from the trees to
the earth to the waters. Second, connected with this: in
this world there is no suffering whatever — one does not
even hear of the 'states of woe'. Indeed, the cosmos itself
is in certain ways absent: 'in this Buddha-field one has no
conception at all of fire, sun, moon, planets,
constellations, stars or blinding darkness, and no
conception even of day and night.'[136] Third, all beings
in this realm are on a course toward Nirvana, and have at
minimum the station of the *Paranirmitavasavartin*
Gods, which is to say, the Gods at the highest station in

the realm of desire (*Kamadhatu*) in the 'vertical cosmology', so whatever they think of, that they obtain, so long as it is good.

It is often thought that the Buddhist teaching of *Sukhavati*, the Pure Land of Amitabha Buddha, appeared only in Japan relatively late in Buddhism, but in fact this is not so: rather, we have here a case, as often in Buddhism, of a pre-existent teaching becoming emphasized due to temporal conditions. Because mankind is passing deeper and deeper into the confusion and error of the *kali yuga*, or dark age of the current world, Buddhism offers a more crystallised and essentialised path to the Truth, in this case the *nembutsu*, or repetition of the Divine Name, in accordance with diminished human capacity. But this path is not new: in the chant entitled 'The Hundred Eight Names of Tara', we find the same doctrine, for the Names are prefaced by the invocatory assertion:

> Listen, you who are greatly endowed and beloved by all beings, to the Names:
> They who correctly repeat them become men of princely wealth,
> Free of all disease, endowed with the virtues of sovereignty,
> Avoiding an ill-timed death, and when deceased, enter Sukhavati.[137]

The verses go on to indicate the countless ways that Tara will bestow upon man not only realisation of the truth, but material wealth and happiness in this world, entry into the Pure Land after death as well. The teachings of *nembutsu*, or recitation of the Divine Names, and of entry into the Pure Land after physical death, are not by any means vulgarisations of the Buddhist doctrine, but rather are traditional doctrines corresponding to *japa*, or recitation of the *mantra* in Hinduism,[138] and to Hesychastic prayer in the Eastern Christian traditions.

The same distinctions which hold to some extent in Christian and Hindu traditions, hold as well in Buddhist tradition: paradise is an indeterminate station on the cosmological scale, a reward for good *karma*, for virtuousness, whereas Sukhavati, or the Pure Land, is a station of being still situated in the cosmos (for it is a 'world-system') but it is beyond the cosmos in that all its inhabitants enter into *nirvana*, into absolute transcendence, and hence it exists wholly within the Buddha-field, is wholly a beneficent 'creation' of the Buddha. It is a 'higher paradise', or an 'expedient heaven', and there is no 'falling back' from it into a human or a subhuman condition.

Thus when we return to the Christian conceptions of paradise and of heaven, we must return again to the saying of Christ that there are many mansions in his Father's house. Though exoterically it is perhaps expedient to believe that heaven is a single station of bliss — and even to argue that the Christian cosmology is not as developed as the Buddhist, say — in fact this is not so, as our quotations from Eckhart, Aquinas and St. Dionysius earlier certainly indicate. Rather, there are many stations of supra-human being, including those of the highest heavens (of complete transcendence in which there is no return to the cosmos, and to suffering) and those of paradise, higher and lower.

But all the possible suprahuman stations of being are still stations of being. Even in the 'expedient heaven' of *Sukhavati*, created by the salvific power of Amitabha Buddha, there are still beings, beings transmuted from a human condition, in a Godlike state and able to obtain whatever desires they wish instantly, in a state of constant delight. But they are still *apparently* beings, even though such a station admits of no return to a lower condition, to a realm of suffering, as do the stations of the Gods. Embraced by the Divine power, beings in this 'expedient heaven' 'ripen' in the Divine light until, wholly transmuted, they are realised as Buddhas themselves, which is to say, they can no longer be termed beings but are wholly inconceivable.

Naturally, there is much in this discussion of heaven and of paradise which has been omitted for various reasons — but our aim here is to sketch the essential aspects of the traditional cosmology and its transcendence. There is after all a traditional cosmology, what we might here call a *cosmologia perennis*, and it is reflected in all the traditions we have here discussed. Be it in Christian, Buddhist, Hindu, Islamic, Egyptian or other terms, spiritual reality and truth are universal, and cannot be otherwise. Likewise, to be human is in an ultimate sense everywhere the same — and it is to the human condition and purpose that we now turn. For no discussion of cosmology would be complete without a discussion of the human place in the worlds.

Chapter VIII
Mankind: The Human Virtuality

In modern times man tends to envision liberation in ever more constricted and materialistic ways. Having almost wholly forgotten the existence of transcendent realms, of anything outside the temporo-physical human sphere, perpetually equating liberation with material equality or with political freedom and the like, modern man seems to be wholly devoid of understanding in the traditional ways. For traditionally, the human purpose is not the accumulation of goods, nor 'material equality', nor even political freedom. Traditionally, liberation is transcendence of suffering, realisation of man's Divine origin.

I realise that what I will say next will no doubt alienate certain of my readers who hold to a scientistic worldview, who hold to the modern prejudice that the material world is everything and that the human purpose lies here, on earth, in the perfection of material consumption. For the traditional doctrines regarding the meaning of human life are completely incompatible with modern evolutionary beliefs, and with the scientistic, manipulative worldview generally.

Of course we are aware of many who would — perhaps not on the scandalous, even ridiculous order of Teilhard de Chardin, but nearly so — attempt to make their religious beliefs correspond to evolutionary doctrines. But these two cannot be made to lie down together, for the evolutionary worldview is fundamentally opposed to and destructive of the religious perspective; one can only force them together by denaturing one's religious understanding until it is meaningless.

The evolutionist hypotheses are so destructive of traditional religious doctrines because they substitute always the human for the Divine order. Ignoring the traditional teachings of timecycles and of the spiritual nature and purpose of the human being, evolutionism necessarily places mankind at the head of a long temporal series of transformations, so that rather than being the Divine vice-regent upon earth, with a 'vertical' origin and purpose, man's origin and purpose is 'horizontalised', making of him merely another animal, with the ability to reason, his very existence 'the result of chance'. To acknowledge any of these elements as being true is to deny the Divine purpose and nature of the human being: to accept them is to deny religion. There are no two ways about it.

One clearly cannot dwell here on this matter, nor is there a need to, any more than there is a need for us to painstakingly attack the increasingly bizarre and untenable theorising of the physicists, for however much certain people might like to imagine similarities between current scientific fancy and traditional cosmological doctrines, there can be no combining the two. The degree with which one accepts the one, is the degree to which one must deny the other. It is not that the physicist's discoveries might not, in some limited way or another, hold true, it is that the physicist's discoveries are necessarily of a different order from the traditional cosmological doctrines, which are revealed to man through transcendent vision, by Divine Grace, and that therefore to focus on things below is to exclude that above, whereas to focus on that above is to illuminate that below. The physicist's discoveries cannot tell man how to live, and what life means. As St. Martin put it, *'Man muss die Dinge durch den Menschen und nicht den Menschen durch die Dinge erklären.'* (One must explain things through man, and not man through things.)[139]

Traditionally man is recognised to be situated so as to conjoin the worlds: he stands on earth, but is the 'pillar' which conjoins heaven and earth. Louis Claude de Saint Martin puts it this way: 'the function of man differs from that of other physical beings, for it is the reparation of the disorders in the universe.'[140] Additionally, 'Man has been placed in the midst of the darkness of Creation only to demonstrate by his native light the existence of a Supreme Agent.'[141] The 'saintly race of man', he says elsewhere, 'engendered from the fount of wonder and the fount of desire and intelligence, was established in the region of the temporal immensity like a brilliant star for the diffusion of a heavenly light.'[142] Finally, 'Man possesses innumerable vestiges of the faculties resident in that Agent which produced him; he is the sign of visible expression of the Divinity.'[143]

All that St. Martin says here is rooted in the teachings of Jakob Böhme, and was in turn reflected in the work of Franz von Baader, who followed after St. Martin: all of these writers to some extent reflect a kind of mystical counterbalance to the advent of Protestantism and rationalism in the West. Essentially, these writers all manifest Christian esoterism and inner vision, thereby calling man's attention back to his cosmological purpose. Man, says St. Martin, is the restorer, meaning that the Fall came about as the result of human miscreance, and so too the Restoration must come about by way of the human centrality in the cosmos. Man is the mediator between God and Creation; he is the Divine vice-regent upon earth, and hence upon him devolves the responsibility for self-transmutation and for restoration of the Paradisal state.

In these doctrines one finds a very real parallel with Buddhism regarding the place and purpose of man in the cosmos: both in the German mysticism and in Buddhist teachings do we find an emphasis upon the essentiality of human transmutation as the means of 'repairing' the cosmos, which is to say, in Buddhist terms, of realising that Transcendence wholly beyond the cosmos and yet permeating it. This we see above all in the representations of the Buddha in Buddhist art: when St. Martin says man is the 'visible expression of the Divinity', he could well have found illustration in the countless Buddha-images seated in their supernal, sidereal peace and splendour, images which always are completely free of the suffering which characterises the human condition, yet bearing the outward form of the human being: they are, in short, the very image of man restored to the Paradisal, transcendent state.

This doctrine of the 'Universal Man' is taught in Islam also, as we can find in the teachings of Abd-al Karim al-Jili, who says:

> Universal Man is the pole around which evolve the spheres of existence, from the first to the last; he is unique as long as existence lasts ... However, he puts on different forms and is revealed by different cults, so that he receives multiple names ...
> Know that Universal Man comprises in himself correspondences with all the realities of existence. He corresponds to the superior realities by his own subtle nature, and he corresponds to the inferior realities with his crude nature ... his heart corresponds to the Divine Throne; and moreover, the Prophet says that the heart of the believer is the Throne of God ...
> Know that the Names of the Essence and the Divine Qualities belong principially to the Universal Man, just as the (universal) kingdom, which he holds by virtue of his essence ... he is then, to God that which the mirror is to the person who examines himself in it ... For God imposed on Himself to contemplate His own Names and Qualities only in Universal Man.[144]

But man is 'ignorant of his own capacity, for he is the place of the Divine pact, and he does not know it.'[145]

The analogy of the mirror here is to be found in all the various traditions: the cosmos is a mirror in which one can see reflected spiritual origin and meaning; and man as microcosmos is also a mirror of the Divine. But man is more than a mirror to the Divine; in a very profound sense he is, at least potentially, pillar of the worlds. That is, in him all Creation is reflected — which means that man can travel both to subhuman and to supra-human realms. This mobility of consciousness could not be unless man possessed within him the possibilities of these realms. One cannot, for instance, imagine an animal or a being in hell ascending to a superior realm while 'rooted' in that station — yet this is possible of man. Hence man is not simply a mirror; he possesses in virtuality the various stations of being.

This universality has its root in complete transcendence: this possibility of complete transcendence, or of realising absolute reality, is the star, or the Divine essence in man which generates all the other possibilities for the human being, and this it is which 'justifies' and sanctifies man. Said Lin Chi (Rinzai) Zenji:

> 'On your lump of red flesh is a true man without rank, who is always coming in and out of the face of every one of you. Those who have not yet proved him, look, look!'
>
> Then a monk came forward and asked: 'What about the true man without rank?'
>
> The Master got down from his seat, seized the monk, and cried 'Speak, speak!'
>
> The monk faltered.
>
> Shoving him away, the Master said: 'The true man without rank: what kind of shit-wiping stick is he!' Then he returned to his quarters. [146]

This 'true man without rank' is Universal Man and yet more than Universal Man. The true man without rank is the essence of the cosmos, and simultaneously that which is wholly beyond the cosmos. Universal Man is man as microcosmos, man as Divine reflection and as sign and seal of the cosmos; but the true man without rank includes and transcends man as microcosmos, being in fact complete transcendence itself. Thus Lin Chi confronts the monk who asks rationally about this true man without rank, trying to make him realise in himself this complete transcendence with 'Speak! Speak!'. And his comment dismissing the true man without rank as 'a shit-wiping stick' is analogous to the 'Speak! Speak!' in that, having tested the monk and found no response, he compassionately shows the way to realisation by demonstrating that the 'true man without rank' is just a concept, just a stick for wiping away shit, human conceptualisation and error.

Eckhart once said that 'I cannot see anything unless it bears some likeness to myself, nor can I know anything unless it is analogous to me.'[1 4 7] By this Eckhart refers to the human need to understand by way of analogy: like must be known by like. Novalis once wrote that only the soul can know the soul, and only God can know God. The 'true man without rank' is an anthropomorphic way of speaking about *dharmakaya*, or the true nature of existence itself as Divine Essentiality. Man must, in order to speak of the transcendent, use *some* terms, and because for man the most convenient and in a certain sense the most accurate are anthropomorphic, as Eckhart acknowledges, then those are used. Man must have before him an image of man having realised the Divine, in order that he know the path to follow and its goal. But this anthropomorphic image of the truth cannot be held to, even as an abstraction like 'true man without rank'. This is the meaning of the 'holy iconoclasm' in Zen Buddhism and particularly in Sufism.

Said Mumon, whose verses are traditionally appended to the *Mumonkan*, the Rinzai Buddhist *koan* (or cases of traditional dialogues) collection:

Before you start to open your mouth,
Your life is already lost!

By this he meant that the instant one begins to speak, one has already entered the world of contingencies and hence of suffering and error. One's true life — the realisation of truth — cannot be verbalised, and yet all the same as a human being one cannot do other than express one's realisation, even if one never says a word. For here is the fundamental dilemma we are trying to represent, and at precisely this point we move from cosmology to metaphysics (for the two cannot be separated, finally): man must express the inexpressible: in this is the reason for all religious tradition. And cosmology depends ultimately upon the inexpressible: it is this which justifies traditional cosmology; it is for this inexpressible realisation that all religion exists, and for that matter the cosmos itself, and mankind. Cosmology is meaningless unless it is rooted in this realisation, so that the whole cosmos is seen to be oriented around it, and existing in order to foster it.

This is why in Islam it is said that the cosmos exists in order that the saint, the *qtub*, the man who has realised the absolute and thereby become the Pole of his generation, may appear. Man is not the center of the cosmos *qua* man, but rather is potentially at the center of the cosmos because of the celestial drama which can be enacted within and by him, because he can ascend 'beyond the worlds' and realise That upon which all the worlds depend. Thus Soen Nakagawa Roshi, a Rinzai Zen patriarch of this century, said to his students:

> THE UNIVERSE IS STANDING RIGHT HERE NOW (BANG)! SEE IT! Okay. We're not sitting in the universe on top of this cushion. The universe itself is sitting. Not you. Not yourself. Nothing else but the universe. But, through our father and mother's first meeting. This is our nearest, most intimate relationship. For each of us. So 'Rinzai was known for his filial piety.' This is important.[148]

Now all of those doctrines or traditions upon which we have touched so far — the Christian, the Islamic, the Buddhist, the Hindu — emphasize time and again both the doctrine of universal man (man as 'sign' and as 'reflection' of the universe, as possessing all the myriad stations in virtuality within himself) and the doctrine of absolute transcendence. Man, in short, is microcosmos: but he is also more than microcosmos. For if he were only the mirror of the celestial, however great his potential powers he would still be perpetually enthralled by the realm of cause and effect, of suffering; only because he can transcend the cosmological stations is man's existence, and the cosmos existence, justified. Without the possibility for transcending it, the cosmos would remain a kind of samsaric prison, which indeed, in the scientistic or materialistic conception, it in fact is.

To the nature of transcendence in traditional religion we now turn, in our final section.

Chapter IX
Transcendence and Liberation

This subject is on the borderline of traditional cosmology in one sense. For though liberation in its nature must have its basis in the cosmos, in the contingent worlds (in that the very word 'liberation' implies a 'movement' from non-liberation, or enslavement), liberation from the cosmological viewpoint must necessarily be 'beyond'. In the vertical cosmology of the Buddhists, liberation is 'above' all the formal and formless stations of being. But nonetheless, in a very real sense, as we have already had occasion to point out, the cosmos itself depends (quite literally) from the Absolute, from that about which nothing can be said. In truth, not only man but the whole of the cosmos was 'projected' in order to manifest, and to realise, this Absolute Reality.

To try to explain the nature of the Absolute is always a paradoxical and ultimately impossible task: one could well say that the world's religions exist in order to express the inexpressible. This inexpressible reality is, in the highest teachings, said to be pure consciousness, and hence in the Tibetan Buddhist 'Book of the Great Liberation' of Padmasambhava, we read:

> When one seeks one's mind in its true state, it is found to be quite intelligible, although invisible.
> In its true state, mind is naked, immaculate; not made of anything, being of the Voidness; clear, vacuous, without duality, transparent, timeless, uncompounded, unimpeded, colourless; not realisable as a separate thing, but as the unity of all things, yet not composed of them; of one taste, and transcendent over differentiation.[149]

Clearly the true state of the mind — the Absolute Truth which is the center of the cosmos, its origin and purpose — must be intelligible, but beyond this one cannot say, for all other characteristics must necessarily be negative. The Absolute must be known, from a physico-temporal perspective, as the negation of the cosmological. Hence the Absolute, or mind in its naked, pure state is not duality, not time, not compound, not coloured, not differentiated, and so forth.

Naturally, this kind of statement — which I could multiply countless times with citations from St. Dionysius the Areopagite, Meister Eckhart, Tauler, Ruysbroeck, Böhme and others in the Christian traditions, as well as from Shankaracarya in the Vedantic tradition, from the Upaniṣads, not to mention Taoist and Islamic sources — is itself conducive to a conceptualisation of the Absolute as negation. And to ward off this kind of error, the Vajracchedika Sutra, or Diamond Sutra, contains the following question-and-answer discussion between Buddha and his disciple Subhuti:

> Subhuti, what do you think? Is the Tathagata to be recognised by some material characteristics?
>
> No, World-honoured One, the Tathagata cannot be recognised by any material characteristic. Wherefore? Because the Tathagata has said that material characteristics are not, in fact, material characteristics.
>
> Buddha said: Subhuti, wheresoever are material characteristics there is delusion; but whoso perceives that all characteristics are in fact no-characteristics, perceives the Tathagata.[150]

That is: one would be wrong to imagine that the Absolute reality exists 'over there', and delusion exists 'here', for although in order to discuss the nature of creation and its relation to the Divine we at times need to use conceptual crutches like that of the Axis of the worlds, in truth characteristics are no-characteristics. The cosmos is itself indivisible from the Tathagata, or Absolute Reality, because the cosmos (all things, all characteristics) in fact has no inherent reality.

Here we enter into the metaphysical doctrine of two truths which was set forth by Nagarjuna in his *Mulamadhyamikakarika*: one has on the one hand ultimate reality, which cannot be expressed in words or concepts, and on the other hand the various skillful means at expressing this truth provisionally. Provisionally, in other words, we can say that the cosmological understanding of the worlds is true; but ultimately even these truths must give way before Absolute Reality.

This is why Dharmaraksita, in his *The Wheel of Sharp Weapons*, says that Yamantaka, or Lord of the Great Death, must trample one's delusions with his two legs, representing the 'two grades of truth': cosmological and metaphysical understanding are both essential to religious progress and final liberation.[151] One must keep in mind the ultimate truth, while realising also that provisional truths also hold so long as we continue in our rounds through the cosmos. Understanding appearance and realising voidness are complementary: intensification of the latter is intensification of the former. The deeper one penetrates into an understanding of Absolute Reality, the more one understands also the cosmological truths. Why is this so? Because the cosmos is itself 'transparent', figuring forth the Divine Mysteries.

The whole of the cosmos is the Divine made manifest; this is the meaning of the Buddhist saying that *nirvana* and *samsara*, absolute and contingent reality, are one. In the *Tetteki Tosui*, or Iron Flute collection of *koan*, we read the following dialogue:

> One day Manjusri stood outside the gate when Buddha called to him. 'Manjusri, Manjusri, why do you not enter?'
>
> 'I don't see a thing outside the gate. Why should I enter?' replied Manjusri.

Manjusri is the bodhisattva of wisdom, and his statement that he sees nothing outside the gate implies exactly this unity of contingent and absolute, of *samsara* and *nirvana.* Manjusri does not go through the gate in order that he might save all beings — and yet is there anything outside the gate to be saved? This is the Mystery.

But these Mysteries cannot be conceived by the ordinary, ratiocinating mind: as Johannes Tauler put it, in his *Spiritual Conferences*:

> It is ... impossible to understand and to follow the process by which the soul is transformed in union with God, losing its own self so that no reason could grasp that this used to be the soul of a created being.
>
> There are some people who are so stupid or so silly that they think this union is a union of nature. They talk about 'being transformed into the divine nature'. This is wicked, untrue and heretical. In the most exalted, most intimate, closest union of man with God, His divine nature and His being are still infinitely beyond every height which man can perceive. It is a divine abyss which has nothing to do with created things. Since it is impossible for any human intellect, however penetrating, to follow the marvelous processes by which food is transformed into us, or to comprehend the excellence of human nature, how can we expect to penetrate this secret abyss which this wonderful food creates in the purest part of illumined souls, especially since the wretched outer man is so feeble and lazy and clumsy in everything he does? This is ... unfathomable.[152]

The *equation* of the human with the Divine is heresy; the human can know of the Divine Abyss, but cannot 'become' it; the human is contingent, and the Divine is Absolute. Nonetheless, this knowing of the human being ('Buddha' means 'knower') is sufficient for the being to wholly transcend the contingent human sphere.

We return to the nature of the Absolute. Meister Eckhart said:

> The divine One is a negation of negations and a desire of desires. What does 'One' mean? Something to which nothing is to be added. The soul lays hold of the Godhead where it is pure, where there is nothing beside it, nothing else to consider. The One is a negation of negations. Every creature contains a negation: one denies that it is the other. An angel denies that it is any other creature; but God contains the denial of denials. He is

that One who denies of any other that it is any thing except himself.[153]

This formulation of the Divine Mystery corresponds to the *koan* quoted above, in that just as Manjusri does not see anything outside the gate — anything that is not Divine in its essentiality — so God as the Divine One is indivisible from the whole of creation.

In one sense the Divine is wholly incommensurate with and indeed even inconceivable from the perspective of Creation; but in another sense the Divine is omnipresent, and closer to the heart of every being than he is to himself. In Upaniṣadic terms, the *atman* at the center of the being is the 'Divine spark', and hence:

> That which is neither internal consciousness nor external consciousness nor both together, which does not consist solely in compact consciousness, which is neither conscious nor unconscious, which is invisible, unapproachable, impalpable, indefinable, unthinkable, unnamable, whose very essence consists of the experience of its own self, which absorbs all diversity, is tranquil and benign, without a second, which is what they call the fourth state — that is the *atman*. This it is which should be known.[154]

In the Satapatha Brahmana we read that:

> One should meditate on Brahman, the truth. Now man possesses insight and, on departing from this world, he will attain the world beyond in accordance with his degree of insight.[155]

Hence:

> One should meditate upon the *atman* which consists of spirit, whose embodiment is life, whose form is light, whose essence is space, which changes its form at will, swift as thought of true resolve and true stability; which contains all odors, all tastes, pervades all regions and encompasses the whole world, speechless and indifferent.[156]

One's station after death corresponds precisely to one's degree of knowledge attained by way of meditation in this life.

But this correlation between the being's degree of meditative realisation and his posthumous destiny (which relationship can also be seen in the Tibetan Buddhist *Bardo Thodröl,* or *Book of the Dead*) can only come about because of the prior Divine emanation of the being. In other words, the being's striving to return to its Divine essentiality corresponds to the emanation of that being in the first place, and its inherent Divine nature. Says Jakob Böhme, the soul yearns for deliverance, for a return to its Divine origin, and:

> So have we likewise to understand the Divine manifestation. For all things have their first beginning from the emanation of the Divine will, whether evil or good, love or sorrow, and yet the will of God is not a thing, neither nature nor creation, wherein there is no pain, sorrow, nor contrary will. But from the efflux of the Word, as by the outgoing of the unfathomable mind (which is the wisdom of God, or the great Mystery, where the eternal understanding is in the temperament) has flowed understanding and knowledge; and this efflux is a beginning of will, when the understanding has separated itself into form. Thus the forms, each in itself, became desirous to have also a counterstroke to its similarity. And this desire is a comprehendingness for selfhood or ownness, as for a place, for a something. And through this something the *Mysterium magnum,* as the unnatural power, is become substantial and natural; and the something has comprehended itself so as to become an individual will. [1] [5] [7]

The Divine emanation, or manifestation, corresponds to the Divine ascent, in that the being must necessarily retrace the 'journey downwards' by ascending. This is why there can be no spiritual realisation (in human terms) without prior human individuation; the manifestation of the individual is the foundation of spiritual realisation.

I mention this correlativity here because it is a central way for understanding our relation to the Absolute: from the human perspective it is at once our Origin and our purpose, and yet the negation of negations. The human being, in other words, needs conceptual 'props' to speak of the Absolute and of its 'journey' towards realisation of that Absolute; but in an ultimate sense there is no such journey, nor is there ultimately a being at all: there is only the Absolute.

But when we consider on the one hand man *qua* man, and on the other the Absolute as complete transcendence even of transcendence, the incommensurability between them brings home once again the necessity for intermediaries, for the hierarchical ascent by which a transmutation of the being can allow a realisation of the Absolute, making the being fit, by way of initiation and meditative practice, for spiritual insight which, were it bestowed without such preparation, would surely blast and disbalance the fragile and limited egoity. It is true that man's suffering arises from ignorance; but it does not follow that this ignorance ought to be obliterated instantly — for man cannot gaze with open eyes upon the Divine Mystery, and were he granted a vision of the Absolute unprepared, he would be destroyed. Rather, just as man's ignorance is the accumulation of slow aeons, so its stripping away is necessarily progressive, until such time as the Divine Light can suddenly pierce within and illumine everything as it truly is.

This is the chief meaning of the controversy, within Mahayana Buddhism, regarding 'sudden' and 'gradual' enlightenment: enlightenment is omnipresent, if one may so speak, and realisation is instantaneous; but at the same time, in order for the being to realise enlightenment it must first be 'prepared'. Were this not so, there could be no such thing as a 'path', for the word would have no meaning and enlightenment would be only a matter of lightning strikes of realisation which struck more or less at random; and certainly this could not be. At this very moment the whole universe is clear and pure, wholly serene and translucent; but we cannot realise this, we cannot fully realise transcendence unless we practise a religious tradition.

The universe itself is indivisible from the Absolute; but we in our ignorance and petty concerns have forgotten this truth: everything in the cosmos figures forth Divine Reality, whether we know it or not. Indeed, the planetary powers, the stars, the trees and birds and grass and waters, all manifest to us the Dharma, the Divine Truth which is our innermost being, and is purity, serenity, enlightenment. Everything symbolises, from an intellectual viewpoint, and in reality *is* Divine Truth. This truth is the foundation of religious practise; it is in fact the foundation of our very being, and it is the impelling force within our entire discussion of traditional cosmology.

Traditional cosmology would have no purpose, indeed would not exist were it not in its variegated entirety pointing toward, bodying forth the Absolute. I have, in these discussions of traditional cosmology, concentrated upon the unity of the disparate traditions, and this is no accident. For though the great religious traditions of the world, naturally enough, each have their own character or essence, or nature, still they cannot but be manifesting the same fundamental truths, and finally the same Absolute, or Ultimate Reality.

Appendix I:
Some Final Words on
Religious Practise

Entry into and practise within a religious tradition during this ending of an age is essential. Some hold that a religious tradition is by no means essential to spiritual realisation. But a religious tradition is man's way for determining that his spiritual practise is not simply a self-delusion. For a religious tradition is far more than simply the continuation of certain rituals or scriptures through time: entry into it is entry into a protective sphere and into a nurturing of realisation which could not occur in isolation from it.

This is particularly important in the modern era, during which delusion permeates the world like a mist, omnipresent and occluding even the most obvious landmarks which, were it only sunny, could easily be seen (things like those I have been discussing in this work). In a golden age, there need be little if anything in the way of a religious tradition, for the simple reason that man is still much more a celestial being, living a long and pure life in the Divine Light, whereas in an era like our own — the *kali yuga* — during which darkness prevails ever more, man needs the transmissive power of a great religious tradition in order to illumine his way, and to reveal that primordial light which, by virtue of our times and our own mental occlusions, is so obscured.

Of course, there is a sense in which the ending of a 'dark age' anticipates the inception of a new era, of the coming golden age, for the seeds of the next cycle are sown in the last. Hence in a curious way there is a correlation between the end and the beginning, this correlation being called *apocatastasis* in the Greek tradition. *Apocatastasis* is the restoration of order. But this anticipation of the coming golden age — connected as it is with the decay of the religious traditions under the erosive power of modernity and of, if we may so speak, the demonic — does not mean that given beings will be 'reincarnated' in the golden age. Rather, there is only a causal connection, symbolised by the traditional implications of seed and of wind, said to connect one timecycle to another.

For man, caught as he is in the downward spiraling of our current age, there is no recourse save to take refuge within the sphere of traditional religion, for the protecting deities of the religious traditions, their angels so to speak, irradiate round man a protective shield, guiding him so that even in this dark era he may be illumined and realise truth. The religious traditions of the world are not a burden, or an opiate, as various fools have called them, but rather are a Divine Mercy, more essential for us the more time accelerates, the more our age races toward its *dénouement*.

Man is called to the tutelage of spiritual guides, of those who have gone before him, and this is only the natural way; one does not learn well, even in a mundane sense, without a teacher, and a teacher presumes a lineage. How much more is this true in the spiritual realm, where the dangers and the possibilities are so much the greater! If we have not the wisdom to submit ourselves to the truth, let us at least not vaunt our errors.

Appendix II:
On the Subtle Being
and the Planets

Astrology is today largely a debased science: separated from its traditional origins and meaning, astrology has in its popular forms become nearly laughable. But even though today its meaning may be obscured, in all traditional cultures astrological knowledge plays a very significant role — astrology has been highly regarded within Hindu, Buddhist, Muslim and Judaeo-Christian traditions, and is also important in the various aboriginal cultures. Indeed, through astrological science within a traditional ambience we can come to understand the warp and weft of the subtle being, or soul, and its relation to the planets and to the cosmos as a whole.

To understand the nature of traditional astrological symbolism, it would probably be best for the Westerner to keep in mind the Platonic concept of archetypal or ideal reality, and its reflection in the temporal world. As Plato said in the famous myth, what we call 'reality' is like flickering shadows on a cave wall or, as in the more traditional symbolism, like reflections in water. Titus Burckhardt wrote in his treatise on mystical astrology:

> The seven planets, which represent the cosmic intermediaries between the immutable world of the archetypes and the earthly centre, actualise, by their combined rhythms and the reciprocal positions which ensue, the spatial relations virtually contained in the indefinite sphere of the sky-limit, the sphere being no other than the totality of the directions of the space and hence the image of the universe.[158]

The sphere which contains the seven planets, in other words, is a reflective *centrum*; it is the image of celestial harmony, the manifestation of the supratemporal in the temporal realm, and is the condensation or fixation, so to say, of the Transcendent.

Man corresponds to the warp and woof, or the harmonic cycles of the seven planets not as a separate *individuum* 'influenced' by their 'rays', as some would have it, but rather as corresponding in his very being itself: the same harmonic cycles which manifest in the planetary cycles, and the tableaux of the stars, manifest in man and form the essence of him.

In order to understand the nature of the planetary symbolism it may be worthwhile, first, to consider some significations traditionally affiliated with the various planets. With the *Sun* is associated open areas, deserts, a physician, a king, a chief minister, tigers, deer, gold, father, effects of good deeds, soul, happiness, prowess, courage, valour, victory in battle, government service, popularity, enthusiasm, sharpness. With the *Moon* is affiliated women, water, herbs, hare, antelope, flowers, agriculture, silver, milk, cows, clothes, meals, health, beauty. With *Mars* is affiliated thievery, battle, rams, cocks, monkey, strength, cruelty, weapons, wounds, and command. With *Mercury* is affiliated scholarliness, astrology, artisanry, learning, the arts, birds, cats, eloquence, intelligence, sacrifice, truthfulness. With *Jupiter* we find treasure, ministerial symbolism, horses, swans, knowledge, virtue, faith, devotion, control over senses, longevity, compassion, royal honour. With *Venus* we find harlotry, bed, music, wealth, dancing, courtesanry, peacocks, cows, clothes, buried treasure, sensuality, prosperity, flowers, passion, festivity, marriage. With *Saturn* we find outcasts, dirtiness, hunters, smithies, death, fear, longevity, degradation, misery, poverty, calumny, sin, censure, misfortune, constancy, iron, debt, lethargy, agricultural implements, prison.

What do these affiliations mean? From the list we can

gather that around each planet are 'clusters' of associated things or beings, each of whom essentially corresponds in some way to the planetary nature. And this correspondence is not random: rather, everything in the cosmos partakes of interrelating symbolic connections. Nothing exists independently — everything reverberates with that which engenders and surrounds it, a truth expressed in Buddhism as *pratityasamutpada*, or codependent origination. Thus we can see how it is that a being, born in a certain time and place, due to certain inclinations manifests given tendencies which in turn correspond to the various 'clusters' or associated energies. But all of this is enormously complex.

So let us imagine a being born under the sign of Taurus, and further say that his ruling planet was Venus. From this we could guess that the being was of a sensual nature, given to a love of certainty and of the earth. But this could well be tempered, in turn, by a strong ascetic inclination in 'balance', so to say, granted by the presence of Saturnian correspondences, also important in the being's energy. Mercury's presence in the chart corresponds to a certain intellectual and communicative tendency: probably the being is a writer or artist. Now all of this is only the barest sketch of possible implications, which can be indefinitely more intricate and complete than this might suggest. But at the least from such an instance we can see how certain planets correspond with certain tendencies.

Of all the planets, the Moon is the most significant both in Western and in Eastern astrology, for the Moon is the 'prism', so to speak, through which the energies of the other planets are refracted. All beings upon earth are sublunary, which is to say also, with Nicholas Culpeper (an astrologer and physician of seventeenth-century England), changeable. Nothing upon earth is constant: all in the sublunary world changes, for, being rather like a reflection in water of the transcendent archetypes, nothing in the material world can possibly be permanent, any more than a reflection in a mirror can be permanent.

As the Moon waxes and wanes (connected as this is with the tides, with water), all creation follows certain cycles: and this is true of all life-cycles. As a result, consultation of the Moon's cycles is essential also for the understanding of illness: the Moon's cycles, being in patterns of seven, correspond to the cycles of illness. Hence the Moon transitting Mars corresponds to choler, as the Moon transitting Saturn corresponds to melancholy, and so forth.[159] The Moon, because of its refractive power, intensifies the 'vertues' or effects of those planets with which it is in conjunction or other relation; hence in medicine, its importance is very great.

But even more generally, the Moon is profoundly important in traditional astrology because its position at birth, and its waxing or waning, correspond very much to the state of the being born, and his future. A child born during a waxing Moon is often fortunate during his life — depending on other factors as well — and conversely, a child born during a waning Moon may often have difficulties. Likewise, many farmers, in the old days before the advent of 'scientific' farming, would plant according to the lunar cycle, and there are still some today who do. One can see why both these instances are so governed: the waxing moon 'pulls' with it the being, and intensifies the virtues exalted at its inception.

The chief principle behind astrological analysis is that the inception of any being or event, corresponding as it does to a particular instant, contains within it the potentiality of that being or event, which one can analyse by understanding the planetary and zodiacal correspondences. Hence, once one understands the fundamental crystallising moment of a given being, one can then analyse that being in accordance with any given future moment, taking into consideration the various interwoven and shifting planetary and zodiacal cycles involved.

In brief: astrology is simply the application of astronomical knowledge to the human realm; astrology is only superstition to the degree that it is employed without a full understanding of the traditional teachings and implications. Now Western astrology tends to be analytical, focusing more upon the psychological and less upon the predictive aspects of life, whereas Eastern astrology tends to be much more specific, worldly, and practical. Of course, one could say that Western astrology is to some extent decapitated by its excessive focus on psychology and subtle balances, whereas Eastern astrology maintains the complete spectrum of human possibilities, ranging as it does from the practical and predictive, to the psychological, to the spiritual. To the degree that Western astrology ignores the former and the latter, is it delimited.

Modern man is conditioned to ignore astrology and to regard it as 'unscientific' — and indeed, regarded from a purely materialistic view, astrology is unscientific, inasmuch as it is not limited to the merely physical. But to ignore something is not to make it untrue; a failure of vision is not proof that things unseen do not exist. At the same time, there is a certain blessing in the relative ignorance of modern man, for his ignorance protects him from himself in certain ways. Modern man's failure of vision corresponds to a freedom from Promethean temptation as well: there is a great deal in traditional wisdom generally which may, being powerful, be used for good or for ill, and since man no longer chooses to be protected by the sphere of traditional religion, nor governed by traditional ethics, it may well be better for him not to know at all.

Still, and with all this in mind, for those who will still enter into the sphere of traditional religion, placing themselves within its protective blessing, there are many riches to be mined from the vast treasures of the world's traditions. Whether one takes as one's source al-Biruni and Islamic tradition, Tibetan Buddhist astrological tradition, Hindu astrological tradition or that Western system employed by Nicholas Culpeper, say, the results will be correspondent to one's knowledge and faith. Astrological understanding can be influential in any aspect of one's life: like all the traditional sciences, its importance is increased in the degree to which it reflects the religious *centrum* of the tradition.

Though astrology is a useful tool, an understanding of it is not the 'one thing needful' in traditional cosmology. My aim in this work was to point out the traditional doctrines of hell, of heaven, of the angels and *asuras*, and above all of man's fundamental purpose — to attain enlightenment. Astrology is useful for balancing one's life, for understanding the nature of the world around us as the figuring forth of the Divine, for understanding ourselves and our destiny or potential. But it is far too complex a subject to do it justice here, and so I included only this appendix, as a brief introduction to a subject I may perhaps address in a longer work.

NOTES

1. By 'traditional' I mean received within a lineage of teachings that stretch back into furthest antiquity, and by 'practise' I mean those ways of living found in the Aboriginal religions, Buddhism, Christianity, Hinduism, Islam, Judaism, and Taoism.
2. Particularly amusing are those 'ecologists' who seem to believe that the earth has evolved man so that he could develop sophisticated communication methods, thereby linking everything on the planet. Of course, technologically astonishing as such communication systems are, they have absolutely nothing to do with spiritual consanguinity; rather, they are a direct manifestation of the modern reliance on technological rather than spiritual needs, corresponding to which are the decreasing privacy available to us all, and the deluge of useless 'information.'
3. *A Basic Call to Consciousness*, Geneva, Switzerland, 1977, p.3. Despite this document's contamination by certain modern political tendencies, it offers a view from a tribal perspective not often available.
4. C.S. Lewis, *The Discarded Image*, Cambridge, 1964, pp.49ff; see also Plato, *Timaeus* 31b, 'it is not possible to combine two things properly without a third to bond them.'
5. *Timaeus* 51
6. G. Scholem, *Kabbalah*, Jerusalem, Keter, 1974, p.129.
7. Brihad Aranyaka Upaniṣad I.4.5
8. See our discussion of the 'fall of the angels' and the nature of the Titans in this volume.
9. This subject has been discussed thoroughly in my *The Alchemy of Healing* (forthcoming). One can see the divorce of traditional medicine from its religious roots in modern Chinese medicine, which attempts to continue herbal and other traditional forms, without the religious culture which engendered and justified them. On this level, it is little better than Western modern medicine.
10. In this regard see James Cowan, 'The World of the Totem' from *Avaloka: A Journal of Traditional Religion and Culture* IV.I & II, Winter, 1989. See also Cowan, *Mysteries of the Dream-time*, Bridport, Dorset, Prism Unity, 1989.
11. James Cowan, 'The World of Totem' *op.cit.*, pp.89-90.

12. Marsilio Ficino, *The Book of Life*, C. Boer, trs., Dallas, Spring, 1988, p.90.
13. *Oeuvres Posthumes* i.102
14. And even what we here call 'special revelation', as in the case of Jacob Böhme for instance, is really within a given tradition and only expands upon certain esoteric aspects of it. Of course, the spirit bloweth where it listeth — but it breathes more easily through the vehicle of a traditional culture, which is after all the very function of tradition.
15. *Gassho*: the Japanese word for two hands clasped, open, palm to palm, as one bows.
16. Maitri Upaniṣad VI, 1-4; VII.11, VI, 35.
17. This limitation to part of one timecycle is evidenced by the abruptness of the Genesis account of Creation, and for the general perplexity with which most Judaeo-Christians must face that account when held against the assertions of scientism, of evolutionism. If the Judaic revelation were complete, it would offer a vaster vision of the cosmic timecycles like that found in the Puranas, for instance, which allows a much stronger denial of evolutionist hypotheses. That there are internal contradictions within the Genesis account is evident from the fact that Cain — though according to the account he is the only remaining son of Adam and Eve — still must bear a mark so that no man shall slay him, and goes on to 'build a city'. Genesis 3: 15, 17. How, if these are the only beings on earth, can one build a city, and what men are there to see the mark? The only answer can be that the Biblical account is attenuated in its focus, looking only to a given lineage and a given part of a timecycle, which is of course our point. Without a wider understanding — either from the Qabala, or from comparative religion — one cannot fully understand Biblical symbolism and meanings.
18. This is why, in the Johannine Revelation, one sees the 'end of time', but as Martin Lings has pointed out, this 'end of time' or Judgment Day corresponds only to the end of a single timecycle, not to the end of temporal cyclicity. The cycles of time continue indefinitely, in vast, vast gyres, as the Hindu and Buddhist teachings regarding *yugas* and *kalpas*, not to mention the *mahakalpas*, affirm, and the Christian apocalypse, like the Tibetan Buddhist myth of the battle for Shambhala, the Kingdom in the North, at the end of this timecycle, corresponds only to the end of one cycle and the beginning of the next, the Golden Age. There are 'cracks' in the Judaic revelation through which one sees the existence of earlier timecycles; this is the meaning, for instance, of the references in Isaiah 34 and

elsewhere to the destroyed kingdom of Edom, which according to Qabalistic interpretation is none other than a civilisation from a previous timecycle, now vanished, and beyond certain temporal 'barriers'. On this point see Leo Schaya, *The Universal Meaning of the Kabbalah*, London, Allen & Unwin, 1971. See also Moshe Idel, *Kabbalah*, Yale University Press, 1988. See also Martin Lings, *The Eleventh Hour*, Oxford, Quinta Essentia, 1988.

19. See Frank Waters, *The Book of the Hopi*, for a discussion of timecycles in Hopi cosmology.

20. See Versluis, *Gateway to Mystery: The I Ching* (forthcoming).

21. See Versluis, *The Egyptian Mysteries*, London, 1988, I.ii.14.

22. Bhagavad Gita VIII.16

23. Jodo Wasan, Hymn 66, based on R. Fujimoto, ed. and trs, Ryukoku University, 1965.

24. See Henry Corbin, *Avicenna and the Visionary Recital*, W. Trask, trs., Princeton, Bollingen, 1960.

25. Chiefly in the Puranas; but rather than seven mountain-rings, there are seven 'ring islands'. For the discussion which follows we relied on R. Kloetzli, *Buddhist Cosmology: From Single World System to Pure Land: Science and Theology in the Images of Motion and Light*, Delhi, Motilal Banarsidass, 1983.

26. Maitri Upanisad VI.4

27. Rg Veda II.11.5

28. See A.K. Coomaraswamy, *Nirmanakaya*, JRAS: 1938, 81-84; see also *Usnisa* and *Chatra, Poona Orientalist*, 3, 1938, p. 403.

29. Genesis III.15

30. See our discussion of this matter a few paragraphs further on.

31. See H.R. Ellis Davidson, *Myths and Symbols in Pagan Europe*, Syracuse University Press, 1988, pp.180ff.

32. Jakob Böhme, *The Three Principles of the Divine Essence*, reprint, Chicago, 1909, Chp.17, no.19.

33. *Ibid*, 17:17

34. *Ibid*, 16:9

35. *Ibid*, 16:48-51

36. *Ibid*, 20:40

37. Mircea Eliade, *Shamanism, op.cit., pp.36ff, 278ff.*

38. *Ibid*

39. We might note here René Guénon's observations, in *The Reign of Quantity and the Signs of the Times*, Lord Northbourne, trs., London, 1953, that shamanism represents, in modern times, a decadent form of the

primordial tradition. But this decadence does not alter the fact that in antiquity shamanism was without question 'complete', and was later absorbed into the highest forms of the various current religious traditions, including the various forms of Tantrism in Tibet, India and Japan. We may say that the essence of shamanism as now known is a complete understanding of cosmology, as a kind of compensation for the forgetting of the metaphysical; this is why it was necessary for shamanism to be absorbed into the revealed religions, that the cosmological understanding may be rejoined with its metaphysical principial origin, without which it quickly degenerates into sorcery.

40. *Commedia, Inferno*, XI.31, 64
41. Majjhima Nikaya, Balapanditasutta
42. Böhme, *op.cit.*, 27:3
43. Revelation 20:15
44. Revelation 21:1
45. See Vendidad II, translated by W. W. Malandra, *An Introduction to Ancient Iranian Religion: Readings from the Avesta and Achaemenid Inscriptions*, Minneapolis, 1983.
46. Cornelius Agrippa, *Of Occult Philosophy*, 2nd ed., London, 1987, Book III, p.477.
47. *Ibid*
48. This is an instance of a transformation from one station to another of such intensity that the earthly state is modified somewhat to conform with it; analogous but inverse is the case when a being 'ascends into heaven', for which transfiguration a 'cloud appears' and the being vanishes entirely from the earthly. There are many instances, in Tibet particularly, of yogis vanishing entirely in closed rooms, leaving behind only their robes and certain 'relics', to use a wholly inadequate word.
49. Naturally, there are yogis who have attained a certain mastery over the physico-temporal elements of existence, and who can be reborn with much of their previous knowledge intact, in order that they continue on the path of religious progress; but once again, it is a matter of certain constituent 'currents' which make up a 'stream of consciousness' continuing on, a relationship between beings which must be conceived in terms of energy transfer. That is: metempsychosis, in this special case, as generally, may be conceived as like one ball hitting another and imparting its motion, or like a stamp being impressed in mud. The lama of the past and the lama present are different beings, linked by a causal chain of particular intensity.

50. Jodo Wasan, *op.cit.*, no.95, p.129, based on the *Muryoju Butsu Myogo Riyaku Daiji Innen Gyo.*
51. Mahaprajnaparamita Sutra, Chp. XIV and XV; see also Kloetzli, *Buddhist Cosmology, op.cit.*, pp.95ff.
52. Frithjof Schuon, *Understanding Islam*, London, Allen & Unwin, 1963, reprint, 1972, Chp. 2, p.80.
53. Origen, *De Oratione* XXIX.13. In Origen may be found not only a clear bridge between Platonist doctrines and Christianity but, by way of the assimilation of his work into the *Philokalia*, a link between Eastern and Western Christianity, and by way of his discussion of metempsychosis, the possibility of correlating Christian and Oriental doctrines.
54. *Ibid*, XXX.2
55. *Meister Eckhart: A Modern Translation*, R.B. Blakney, New York, Harper, 1941, Chp. VIII, p.137.
56. *Ibid*, I.12, p.18
57. Thus Dogen Kigen Zenji, when he died, said he was going straight to hell, not because he had committed sins worthy of that, by any means, but because he wished to liberate all beings, and where is liberation more needful than in hell? Unless we are willing to say that ignorance is eternal, we have to concur that what it engenders — hell — also is not eternal. In a real sense, ignorance is the negation of the eternal.
58. René Guénon, *The Multiple States of the Being*, Joscelyn Godwin, trs., Burdett, 1984, p.21. The motivation to escape hell leads only to a station of bliss 'above' the human, a station which only possesses a contingent reality.
59. Genesis I.6-7.
60. See Brhadaranyaka Upaniṣad I.2.1, trs. by A.K. Coomaraswamy, in *The Vedas: Essays in Translation and Exegesis*, London, Prologos, 1976, pp.7-8, 124.
61. Platonism represents a truncated religious understanding, being the condensation or even, in a certain sense, the residue of the Greek Mystery tradition, which derived from the Egyptian. Hence Platonism has a certain ability to seed the understanding in Western tradition, and preserves a delimited religious understanding, a kind of traditional cosmology in the West (along with Hermeticism) but without a correspondent means of realisation, being in essence an intellectual understanding of doctrine. As such it is useful in some respects, but is not a path in itself; hence for example Ficino and Pico both, in their divergent ways, had to take refuge in Christendom.
62. Coomaraswamy, *op.cit.*, p.9.

63. See Adrian Snodgrass, *The Symbolism of the Stupa*, Ithaca, SEAP, 1985), *passim*.
64. See René Guénon, *The Reign of Quantity and the Signs of the Times*, London, 1953.
65. Early in a given timecycle, man and the extrahuman beings are in communication, even being able to cohabit, as when the giants or *asuras* 'laid with women' in the Biblical record we shall discuss shortly. As man's mentality hardens against the Divine, as the timecycle proceeds, man also loses his capacity to contact beings in the subtle realms, extrahuman beings. Thus the realms of faery are forgotten, or ignored, for instance.
66. Surah 72:1-16
67. *Ibid*
68. Ko Hung, *Nei P'ien*, James Ware, trs., Cambridge, 1966, 17: 6b
69. *Ibid*, 17:7a
70. Agrippa, *op.cit.*, Book III, Cap. XXXIII, p.450.
71. *Ibid*, Book III, Cap. XXXIV, p.453.
72. *Ibid*, p.450
73. Böhme, *Sexta Theosophica Puncta*, VI.15.
74. *Ibid*, VI.18
75. *Ibid*, VI.25
76. Dualism is, in a limited way, true: Taoism for instance is by no means dualistic, the Tao being one, but still it recognises the primordial 'opposed' powers of yin and yang. One has to understand the cosmos before one can transcend it; one has to realise that duality governs our world, before we can realise unity. Those scholars who would attack Persian dualism, for instance, simply do not understand that an awareness of cosmological dualism does not entail a denial of metaphysical unity.
77. Henry Corbin, *Cyclical Time and Isma'ili Gnosis*, London, Kegan Paul, 1983, p.44.
78. See Martin Lings, *The Eleventh Hour*, London, Quinta Essentia, 1987.
79. See Rg Veda X.90.13; see also Artharva Veda XI.4.15.
80. See our discussion of apocatastasis in *Avaloka: A Journal of Traditional Religion and Culture*, II.ii, 1988.
81. See Eliade, *Yoga: Immortality and Freedom*, Princeton, 1968, p.138.
82. See Danielou, *Hindu Polytheism*, New York, 1964, p.141; see also Mahabharata 12.8.381.
83. Mahabharata I.6.58.1-35.
84. Mahabharata I.6.58.45ff.
85. Mahabharata I.16.(201).1, 'Sunda and Upasunda'.

86. Shankaracarya, *Commentary on the Chandogya Upaniṣad* I.2.1.
87. King Gylfi did not go by his proper name on the principle that to give away one's proper name on a magical journey is to give the key to one's own destruction.
88. Voluspa, 7-9; see also *The Elder Edda*, O. Bray, trs., London, 1908.
89. Voluspa, 21
90. Voluspa, 29-30
91. Voluspa, 40-42; see also Grimnismal, 39.
92. Grimnismal, 39, 52
93. Henry Corbin, *Cyclical Time and Isma'ili Gnosis, op.cit.*, pp.177-8.
94. Scholem, *Kabbalah*, Jerusalem, 1974, p. 124.
95. This is the fundamental basis of theurgy: sorcery, on the other hand, consists in joining that which should not be joined; whereas fundamentalist religion consists in separating that which should not be separated. The former consists in an absence of moralism; the latter consists in its overabundance.
96. Enoch here corresponds to Hermes, the 'messenger of the Gods'; and indeed there are many points of correlation between the Enochian revelations and the Hermetic.
97. *Enoch*, XV.1-XVI.4, London, 1917, R. Charles, trs.
98. *Enoch* VII.1
99. *Enoch* VIII.1ff.
100. *Enoch* I.IX.1
101. *Enoch* X.14
102. See Grimm, *Teutonic Mythology*, London, 1888, vol. IV.1336ff.
103. *Enoch*, CVI.1
104. *Enoch* LXXXIX.1
105. Black is corruption (the *Kali-yuga*); white is the 'golden age' or *Krita yuga*, of which the *Dvipara yuga* is a reflection; and red is the colour of the *Treta yuga*, or third age. This corresponds to the alchemical work, black being the state of corruption, red being the fire of purification, white being the state of purity.
106. *Enoch*, LXXXVIII.3
107. *Enoch*, XVI.1
108. Guénon, *The Reign of Quantity and the Signs of the Times*, London, 1953, pp.206-7.
109. 'Baraita de Ma'aseh Bereshit', anonymous, trs. D. Meltzer, from *The Secret Garden*, New York, 1976, pp.14ff.
110. *Myths and Legends of China*, E.T.C. Werner, London, 1922.
111. *Odyssey*, 11.577, 11.307.

112. *Inferno*, 31.58-66
113. Guénon, *The Reign of Quantity and the Signs of the Times, op.cit.*, p.207.
114. See on this point Versluis, *Gateway to Mystery: The I Ching* (forthcoming).
115. St. John of the Cross, *Spiritual Canticle*, Stanzas of the Bride and Bridegroom, I.8, Commentary, in *The Collected Works of St. John of the Cross*, K. Kavanaugh, O.C.D., trs., New York, 1964, p.465.
116. St. Dionysius the Areopagite, *Cel. Hier.* Cap. IV.
117. *Ibid*
118. Plotinus, *Enneads*, II.9, 'Against the Gnostics'.
119. Ibn Arabi, *Fusus al Hikam, The Wisdom of the Prophets*, trs. Titus Burckhardt, London, 1975, p.76.
120. See, for instance, Nicholas Culpeper, *Astrological Judgment of Diseases From the Decumbiture of the Sick*, London, 1655. Culpeper endured enormous abuse as a result of his efforts to reinstitute traditional medicine in the West, medicine based to a considerable degree upon astrological science. For Eastern works see those of Dr. Yeshe Donden, Terry Clifford, and our own *The Way of Healing*, which draws on both Eastern and Western traditions.
121. René Guénon, *The Multiple States of the Being*, Burdett, 1984, Chp. 13, p.106.
122. Titus Burckhardt, *Mystical Astrology According to Ibn Arabi*, B. Rauf, trs., London, Beshara, 1977, Cap. III, p. 26.
123. Pico della Mirandola, *Heptaplus*, Cap. III, D. Carmichael, trs., Indianapolis, 1940, reprint 1965), p.110.
124. St. Dionysius the Areopagite, *Cel. Hier. op.cit.*
125. See Kloetzli, *Buddhist Cosmology, op.cit.* p.29; see also La Vallée Poussin, *L'Abhidarmakosa de Vasubandhu*, 7 vols. 1923-1931, cap. iii, p.159.
126. Kloetzli, *op.cit.*, p.34.
127. St. Dionysius, *Cel. Hier. Cap.* VII.
128. *Ibid*
129. Bhagavad Gita, V.25
130. *Ibid*, IX.21; see also R. Panikkar, *The Vedic Experience: Mantramanjari*, London, 1977, p.640.
131. I abbreviate this discussion here because I have already given much more elaborate consideration to the Egyptian understanding of heaven and of paradise in Versluis, *The Egyptian Mysteries*, London, 1988.
132. A.K. Coomaraswamy, *The Vedas: Essays in Translation and Exegesis*, London, 1976, p.69.
133. Chandogya Upaniṣad VIII.6.6.5
134. Aquinas, *Summa Theol.* I.Q. 108, A.8.

135. Eckhart, quoted by Coomaraswamy, *op.cit.* p.72.
136. Sukhavativyuha, 15-27, trs. E. Conze, in *Buddhist Texts Through the Ages*, New York, Harper, 1964.
137. *Arya-Tara-nama-ashtottara-shataka-stotra*, ed. G. de Blonay, *Matériaux pour servir à l'histoire de la déesse bouddhique Tara*, 1895, pp.48-53.
138. This is not to say that all *japa* in Hindu traditions are intended to result in rebirth in a Pure Land — clearly this is not so. We only suggest that the means — recitation of the Name — is the same among the various traditions.
139. St. Martin, from *Des erreurs et de la vérité ou les hommes rappelés au principe universel de la science, par un philosophe inconnu*, Lyon, 1775, quoted by Franz von Baader, *Sämtl. Werke*, VIII.59.
140. St. Martin, *Tableau Naturel*, Part I, p.55.
141. *Les Voies de la Sagesse, Oevres Posthumes*, i.68.
142. *Le Ministère de l'Homme-Esprit*, p.162.
143. *Tableau Naturel*, pp.57-8.
144. Abd al-Karim al-Jili, *Universal Man*, trs. by Titus Burckhardt, Sherbourne, 1983, p.xx.
145. *Ibid*
146. *The Record of Lin Chi*, R.F. Sasaki, trs., Kyoto, 1975, p.3.
147. *Meister Eckhart: A Modern Translation*, R. Blakney, trs, New York, 1941, p. 148.
148. *The Soen Roku: The Sayings and Doings of Master Soen*, New York, 1986, p.23.
149. *The Tibetan Book of the Great Liberation*, W.Y. Evans-Wentz, ed., Oxford, 1954, p.211.
150. Vajracchedika Sutra, Section V.
151. Dharmaraksita, *The Wheel of Sharp Weapons*, commentary, Geshe Ngawang Dhargye, Dharamsala, 1978, st. 50, p.18.
152. J. Tauler, *Spiritual Conferences*, E. Colledge, trs., St. Louis, Herder, 1961, Sermon XXXII, p.268.
153. *Meister Eckhart*, Blakney, trs., *op.cit.*, p.247, fragment 41.
154. Mandukya Upaniṣad 7
155. Satapatha Brahmana X.6.3.1
156. *Ibid*
157. Jakob Böhme, *Six Theosophical Points*, *op.cit.*, *Theoscopia*, 23.
158. Titus Burckhardt, *Mystical Astrology According to Ibn Arabi*, Gloucestershire, 1977, p.26.
159. Nicholas Culpeper, *Semiotica Utanica, or Culpeper's Judgement of Diseases*, London, 1662, p.2.

Ecstatic Ritual
Practical Sex Magic
Brandy Williams

FROM ancient temple dwellers to modern urban residents, priests, poets and people of all walks of life have looked to sexuality to aid them in connecting with the Divine.

In a subject previously obscured by foreign terms and deliberate 'blinds' for the uninitiated, ECSTATIC RITUAL offers the reader clear, concise exercises and ritual forms which comprise a full understanding of sacred and magical sexuality. Heterosexual, gay and lesbian workers, in couples or singly, explore a magical system which methodically explains the worship and union of the Divine within each person.

BRANDY WILLIAMS, who has worked as a professional journalist and freelance writer, has written articles and taught workshops on the subject for a number of years. She has been

a Priestess and Historian of the Western Mysteries for over 15 year

8½ x 5½, 160 pp
Full colour cover
Diagrams and line illustrations
1 85327 051 2 Paperback

Aphrodisiacs and Love Magic

The Mystic Lure of Love Charms

Pamela Allardice

TAKE control of your love life — with a little practical magic. Pamela Allardice looks at traditional love lore — omens to observe, games to play, potions to prepare and the most auspicious days for amatory progress. In particular, she examines powerful plants, herbs, fruits and flowers which may be enlisted to help love along. From exotic tropical love plants to traditional cottage flowers, from symbolic flowers used to bedeck Oriental bridal chambers to herbs employed by French and Italian bridegrooms to fortify themselves for the night ahead.

This is the first time that such a thorough study has been made of the lovely nonsense that makes the world go round. Although few people today would use potions and divination to solve the problem of who they are to marry, many lovers still seek lucky omens and observe ancient customs, albeit without being aware of their significance.

8½ x 5½, 128 pp
Full colour cover
1 85327 031 8 Paperback

Hallucinogens

Cross-Cultural Perspectives
Marlene Dobkin de Rios

THIS book surveys the uses of mind-altering plants in eleven societies in the Americas, Asia, Africa, Australia, and New Guinea, ranging from the hunter-gatherer level to the complex ancient civilizations of the Aztec, the Maya, the Nazca, the Mochica, and the Inca. Some of the data are derived from the author's research in modern Peru, where plant hallucinogens are used in folk healing. Many other data have been assembled from a variety of scientific and anthropological publications. The lay reader with a general interest in primitive ritual, religion, and healing will find a great deal of information in this concise volume, which is illustrated with drawings of the various plants that can produce altered states of consciousness and with reproductions of ancient Peruvian art that the author sees as drug-related.

Several themes emerge from de Rios's cross-cultural examination of sacred plants. She argues convincingly that plant hallucinogens, which have been used from time immemorial, influenced human evolution. She also discusses religious beliefs that may have been influenced by the mind-altering properties of particular plants, and she focuses on the ways hallucinogens have influenced ethical and moral systems.

MARLENE DOBKIN DE RIOS is professor of anthropology at California State University.

8½ x 5½, 256 pp
Full colour cover
Line drawings and tables
1 85327 061 X Paperback

GATEWAY TO INNER SPACE

SACRED PLANTS, MYSTICISM
AND PSYCHOTHERAPY

Edited by
CHRISTIAN RÄTSCH

ateway
Inner Space

cred Plants, Mysticism
d Psychotherapy

. Dr. Christian Rätsch

 recent years there has been
onsiderable debate about the
onary experiences induced by
ucinatory plants — often
rded as sacred in shamanic
eties — and the related use of
hedelics in contemporary
chology.

s fascinating work consists of
ys by many leading researchers
he field of altered states of
sciousness — presented to honour
Albert Hofmann, who first
overed the extraordinary effects
SD in 1943.

ured here are writings on the
ical use of psychedelics, the
roversial issue of 'molecular
ticism', the relationship of
aments to Gnosis, death and

rebirth themes in shamanism,
comparisons between meditative and
psychedelic experiences and states of
tryptamine consciousness.

Among the many distinguished
contributors to this remarkable
volume are Dr Stanislav Grof,
Terence McKenna, Dr Ralph
Metzner, Professor Hanscarl Leuner,
Dr Claudio Naranjo, Claudia Müller-
Ebeling and Dr Christian Rätsch.

DR CHRISTIAN RÄTSCH is an authority
on sacred plants and the culture of
the ancient Mayans. He has
published extensively in German —
his books include *Chactun — die
Gotter der Maya* and *Bilder aus der
unsichtbaren Welt.*

8½ x 5½, 256 pp
Full colour cover
1 85327 037 7 Paperback

The Celtic Twilight

Myth, Fantasy and Folklore
W.B. Yeats

ALTHOUGH renowned as one of the most famous poets of the 20th century, WILLIAM BUTLER YEATS (1865–1939) was also a devoted exponent of the western mystical and magical traditions. Yeats met with students of the occult in Dublin in the 1880s and was later introduced by his friend Charles Johnson to the Theosophical Society. Yeats subsequently left the Theosophists and in 1890 was initiated as a ceremonial magician of the Golden Dawn — arguably the most influential esoteric order in the western magical tradition — and for a time became its leader.

Yeats exercised a profoundly Celtic influence on his fellow occultists and his love of Irish folklore is reflected in this book, which was first published in 1893. THE CELTIC TWILIGHT brings together many of Yeats' most enchanting and mystical tales — a dazzling array of sorcerers faeries, ghosts and nature spirits which draw their inspiration from the visionary heart of Irish folk tradition.

This book is a special tribute to the memory of W.B. Yeats and is published fifty years after his death

8½ x 5½, 128 pp
Full colour cover
1 85327 029 6 Paperback

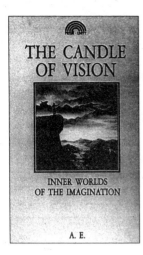

he Candle
f Vision

ner Worlds
the Imagination

E. (George Russell)
REWORD BY Nevill Drury

IRST published in 1918, this book
is one of the classics of modern
tern mysticism. While it may
m that such concepts as 'creative
ialisation' and 'imagining our own
ity' are recent innovations of the
nan potential movement, they are
found here — in a very lucid
eloquent form.

author was a distinguished
ter, artist and poet and believed
t each of us can use the creative
ers of the imagination as a
hway to other worlds. The
gination can transport us to an
some, mystical universe and we
n sense the vastness of the
nite. This is the true nature of
visionary inspiration.

A.E. was the *nom de plume* of
GEORGE RUSSELL (1867–1935).
Russell was a major literary figure in
the Irish Renaissance and a friend of
W.B. Yeats. Like Yeats, Russell was
strongly influenced by theosophical
mysticism and by the beauty of
Celtic mythology. He was the author
of several works, including *Song and
its Fountains* and *The Avatars*, but
CANDLE OF VISION is widely regarded
as his masterpiece.

8½ x 5½, 112 pp
Full colour cover
1 85327 030 X Paperback

Exploring the Paranormal

Perspectives on Belief and Experience

EDITED BY Prof. G.K. Zollschan, Dr J.F. Schumaker and Dr G.F. Walsh

THIS important anthology brings together some of the world's leading authorities in their fields and presents frameworks for understanding paranormal belief and experience. It describes special applications of the scientific method and also features debates between believers and unbelievers in the paranormal. There are chapters on mind-expanding drugs, the near-death experience, mysticism and meditation, an evaluation of the contribution of biology to the study of the paranormal, and an examination of 'miracles'.

Contributors to this far ranging book include such internationally acc-

laimed figures as Charles Tart, Stanley Krippner, Harvey Irwin, Anthony Flew, and John Beloff as well as many other distinguished researchers from the United States, Britain and Australia.

The three editors also differ in their views. *ZOLLSCHAN* is a sociologist and practising Jewish mystic. Formerly an assistant to Sir Karl Popper he has taught in the USA, Canada, Britain and Australia. *SCHUMAKER* is a clinical psychologist and is an "absolute unbeliever" in the paranormal. *WALSH* is a social scientist and Roman Catholic with an interest in how inter-denominational differences affect belief in the supernatural.

8½ x 5½, 400 pp
Full colour cover
1 85327 026 1 Paperback

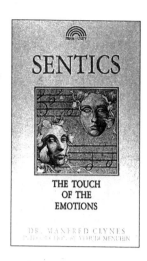

entics

e Touch of the Emotions
 Manfred Clynes

RODUCTION BY
hudi Menuhin

ENTICS reveals how emotions are
 communicated early in life and
nusic, painting and sculpture. It
 revolutionary, new scientific
:ipline which examines the
:ogical basis of emotion. Its
:overer, DR MANFRED CLYNES, is
 inventor of the Sentograph, an
:nious device which measures
ttional responses through the
:ertips. Clynes' research has also
overed genetically programmed
n and nervous system patterns
 such basic emotional states as joy,
:r, hate, grief and love. Moreover
las developed the so-called 'Sentic
les', an exercise technique for the
▸tions, which anyone can learn
 which can lead to a profound
:e of well-being.

The author is one of the most
creative, multidisciplinary minds
working in science today. He holds
advanced degrees in neuroscience,
engineering and music. He is a
university lecturer and has toured
Europe as a concert pianist.

"This breakthrough could only have
been achieved by a musician . . . a
scientist who remains a musician at
heart." Yehudi Menuhin.

8½ x 5½, 284 pp
Full colour cover
1 85327 025 3 Paperback

PRISM · UNITY

MODERN RITUAL MAGIC

THE RISE OF
WESTERN OCCULTISM

FRANCIS KING

Modern Ritual Magic

The Rise of Western Occultism

Francis King

THIS is the inside story of the Hermetic Order of the Golden Dawn and associated occult offshoots — told in its entirety for the first time. The author's researches into the conflict between W.B. Yeats and Aleister Crowley are described in detail, as well as the full story of Yeats' early magical training and practices. Francis King also relates the often difficult relationship between Yeats and the influential Kabbalist, Macgregor Mathers.

However, it is not only the student of the Golden Dawn who will find this book absorbing. King also describes Rudolph Steiner's attempt to take over English occultism and links Bengali Tantricism with the magic of the American Mulatto. All the major figures in modern western magic feature in this book, which since its first publication in 1970, has been rightly regarded as one of the major histories of the western esoteric tradition.

FRANCIS KING is also the author of *Magic: the Western Tradition, Sexuality Magic and Perversion* and *The Secret Rituals of the O.T.O.* He co-authored *Techniques of High Magic* with Stephen Skinner.

8½ x 5½, 224pp
Full colour cover
1 85327 032 6

Primitive Magic

The Psychic Powers of Shamans and Sorcerers

Ernesto de Martino

THE idea of magic challenges our basic concepts of reality and the natural order of things. But for native shamans and sorcerers magic is as tangible and 'real' as science is in our modern 'civilisation'. The Australian Aborigine, for example, will die if pierced by an arrow that has been 'sung' — no matter how superficial the wound.

This astounding book describes societies where magic is a way of life, where sorcerers, shamans, diviners and fire walkers form powerful bonds with the psychic realities of Nature.

PRIMITIVE MAGIC is itself an initiation into the enthralling world of ancient mysteries.

'There is no such thing as unreality; there are only various forms of reality' — Eugene Ionesco

ERNESTO DE MARTINO lives in Rome and is Professor of the History of Religions at Cagliari University. He has a long-standing interest in the links between parapsychology and anthropology and is the author of several works in this field, including *South Italy and Magic* and *Death and Ritual in the Ancient World*.

8½ x 5½, 192 pp
Full colour cover
1 85327 021 0 Paperback

Visionaries and Seers

They Saw Tomorrow

Charles Neilson Gattey

8½ x 5½, 288 pp
Full colour cover
1 85327 020 2 Paperback

I N this unique book, Charles Nielson Gattey recounts the stranger-than-fiction life-stories of the most astounding seers and sorcerers of all time. Such well-known characters as Nostradamus and Cheiro are here in all their brilliant and bizarre detail — including the former's visions of the Second World War and a bleak outlook for Britain towards the end of the 20th century and the latter's predictions of Edward VIII's romance and abdication — as well as such lesser-known but equally intriguing figures as Mlle Lenormande, clairvoyante and confidante of the Empress Josephine and Ernst Krafft, alleged by some to have been Hitler's personal astrologer.